Following My
Dreams

Garland W. Yarborough, MD, FACG, FACP

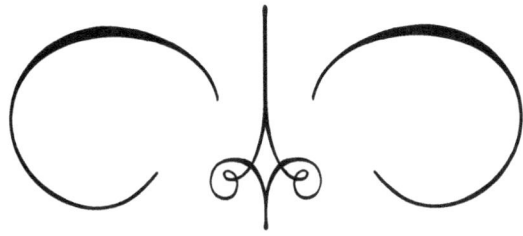

Following My
Dreams

ARPress
ILLUMINATING IDEAS
EMPOWERING VOICES

ARPress
45 Dan Road Suite 5
Canton, MA 02021

Hotline: 1(888) 821-0229
Fax: 1(508) 545-7580

Ordering Information:
Quantity sales. Special discounts are available on quantity purchases by corporations,associations, and others. For details, contact the publisher at the address above.

Printed in the United States of America.

ISBN-13:   Softcover   979-8-89356-572-0
            eBook   979-8-89356-573-7

Library of Congress Control Number: 2024903104

TABLE OF CONTENTS

To those individuals who aspire to fulfill their dreams that seem unattainable to others and are willing to work hard and persevere even in the face of a major adversity

This manuscript covers my birth to my graduation from Salina public schools.

The next manuscript will cover college through medical training at Wake Forest Medical School, Northwestern, and Vanderbilt. A third manuscript will cover graduation from medical school and medical training until the present.

PROLOGUE

Every morning, Mom and I would escort Sissy to be picked up by Ms. Bunnel, her first-grade teacher. Ms. Bunnel was a very kind teacher that almost everybody wanted their children to be taught by her.

This was in contrast to the other first-grade teacher. There were a lot of bad stories circulating about Ms. Eggleston, which were later proved to be true. I never got a ride to school. We had to make sure that Ms. Bunnel was the one picking up Sissy. Ms. Bunnel picked up Sissy because of her asthma. Sissy would occasionally get shortness of breath with wheezing. If these episodes were not stopped with shots or inhalers, she would have to be admitted to the hospital. Ms. Bunnel was a very good and caring teacher. Ms. Eggleston, the other first grade teacher, was a cranky old lady. I never saw her laugh or grin. Unfortunately, I was selected to be in Ms. Eggleston's class.

The very first day, she went over the rules and regulations. She pulled out her paddle to show us what we would get if we disobeyed her rules. We could tell by her expressions that she seemed gleeful when showing the paddle to the class.

Our school was a large room divided by a partition that could be passed to allow two different classes. One could occasionally hear sounds coming from the other classroom; certainly, when a student got a paddling in Ms. Eggleston's room, it could be heard easily in the other room. At recess, everybody knew who the student was and why they got the paddling. Our school also had a small outside area for playing at recess. We could not play softball or hardball very well because of the limited playing area. There was a small swing set. We had an outside toilet. We had water from an outside well with a large handle that we had to pump in order to get water. The water was cold and excellent.

One of our rules was we were not supposed to go off the school grounds. This made it difficult if we were playing softball. After one week from the start of school, we had a math test. I did not understand math at all. Ms. Eggleston was not the type of teacher we could go and get help from if we did not understand a concept. I would be terribly embarrassed if the class knew my stupidity regarding math. I could see Georgia Gann's test answers very well. She was a smart girl. I was just about through copying the math test when Ms. Eggleston slapped me with a plastic ruler on my right arm. The anxiety was terrible. I was told to come to the front of the class. I had to tell the class what I was doing. I received twelve slaps with the paddle that had holes in it. The holes were supposed to make the paddling hurt more. It was horribly painful. Not only was this painful, but also it was very embarrassing. I walked out the front door and went to the railroad tracks.

Walking north on the railroad tracks seemed to bring me solace for a while. I know we were not supposed to go off school grounds, but I had to do that in order to regain my composure. I did not want my class seeing me cry from the pain. The class shunned me for the next three to four weeks.

Within a week, I was shooting hoops by myself. This kid started making fun of the holes in my shoes. I chased him down and hit him in the nose. Immediately his nose started bleeding profusely. He ran to Ms. Eggleston, crying with a bloody nose. Blood was everywhere. This kid was not disciplined at all. He got a cold cloth and was told to go to his seat. At the beginning of the class, Ms. Eggleston told me to come to the front of the class. She asked the class if fighting was one of those rules that we were not supposed to do. The class, in unison, said yes. Ms. Eggleston asked me what I did. I told the class I hit Rick in the nose with my fist. Ms. Eggleston asked me why I did this. I replied because he was making fun of the holes in my shoes. How embarrassing was this? Now, if the class did not know before that I had holes in my shoes, they knew it now. I could not help it; that was all I had. Ms. Eggleston told me to bend over as she gave me twelve slaps with the paddle. My buttocks had not yet recovered from the last one. The paddling was worse than the first one. I immediately went out the front door and again went to the railroad tracks and the river. I was crying because of the pain. I felt used; my self-esteem was gone. And again, the school shunned me at recess. I had to play by myself, which was fine with me. When I got home, I went to the hay house, where my dogs were. I knew my dogs loved me. Mom soon came to the hay house. I told her that I got another paddling at school. I told Mom this kid was making fun of the holes in my shoes. I told Mom that the other kid was not disciplined at all. This made Mom very mad. Mom told me to come to the kitchen. I showed her my buttocks. There was a lot of swelling and bruising, and it was tender. Mom told me she was going to school with me tomorrow. Mom was mad as hell. She told Ms. Eggleston about how my buttocks were swollen and bruised and that I was having a lot of pain. Mom was getting in Ms. Eggleston's face. Mom asked her if this was what she intended to do to a kid when she paddled them. She asked Ms. Eggleston, "Do you know what this is, what you are doing when you paddle someone? Answer me!" Ms. Eggleston was stunned and embarrassed as the class was watching all of this. Mom asked her, Ms. Eggleston, why she paddled and Ms. Bunnel never did. Ms. Eggleston had no explanation. Mom told her that she was going to talk to Mr. Pierce, the principal, about her. Mom told her that she had better have a damn good reason if she paddled again. If there was anything good that came out of this, it was that the number of paddling that Ms. Eggleston gave markedly decreased, at least for that year. Instead, she adopted Ms. Bunnel's form of disciplining. I think she knew that the two paddlings that she gave me were a very harsh treatment producing a lot of pain, swelling, and bruising in addition to the anxiety produced with the class watching me getting a paddling, which was way beyond the pale. After these two paddlings, I could not sit for a long time. Sitting for a long time produced a lot of pain in my buttocks. I would frequently get up from my desk and go get a drink of water. I dared this cranky old bitch to say something. I would tear into her, and it would not be pretty.

One day after school, instead of going home, I grabbed the basketball and went out and shot hoops. I waited until all the cars were gone. I went back into the school to put the basketball up. There was nobody around. I opened the desk, and there was the paddle. I grabbed it and carried it under my coat. I took it and put it in the hay house to be buried in the metal building in our backyard. The next day at school, Ms. Eggleston was very mad because her paddle was gone. She probably suspected me but could not prove it. Before long, she got another paddle. I did not get another paddling for the rest of the year in first grade. These two paddlings were not the last ones I ever got. Indeed, I received several more. I remember Mom telling Ms. Bunnel that I had to go to college.

I asked Mom what college was. Mom said it was a place people went to learn how to be a teacher, doctor, lawyer, engineer, and so on. She said I could ask my teacher what it was, and they could explain it better. If college was so important, why was it not important for Mom and Dad? Mom did stay with a family in Pryor so she could graduate from high school. After graduation, Mom and Dad were ready to get married, and that is what they did. Having no transportation and no money sealed their fate as far as not going to college.

This college thing was suspect on many fronts. I asked Mom if I would have to leave her as I began to cry. She told me, "Yes," as we lay on the floor for our daily nap. It was thought that a nap would help prevent polio, so Mom made us take an hour nap every day.

I loved Mom. After our daily nap, we would walk, holding hands, to this dilapidated gas station. Looking at this station, one would think it was toxic, and it probably was.

There was a four-by-six-foot box filled with pop, which was bathed in ice cold water. Mom would get a Coke, and I would get an RC Cola. I would get a peanut patty, and Mom would get a Milky Way. The man behind the counter would open our drinks so we could eat and drink our treats. We would walk home slowly. This is the same man that told me that used motor oil would get rid of the mange. He gave me all the motor oil I needed. Indeed it did. This is also the place where I had to carry a five-gallon can to get kerosene for the stove in the kitchen.

My first four years of grade school, I learned very little. Both math and reading were difficult for me. Mom helped me a lot. I would do math and reading every night with her. I was learning a lot more with Mom than I was with the teachers. The fourth-grade teacher that taught only music was a disaster.

I started turning things around in the fifth grade. I would get books about rockets, the universe, medicine, math, and I loved it. The library in our school was nonexistent. I began to surpass everybody in class in everything. I was excelling not only academically but also in sports. I was playing basketball with the seventh and eighth grade. We had several tournaments that were fun to play in.

The year that I saw baseball at the grade school, I was so impressed that I told myself I was going to be the catcher the next year. Indeed, at next year's tryouts, I was the starting catcher. Everybody was so impressed with my athletic abilities as a catcher they wanted to be around me as much as they could. Now, it was my turn to shun them, and I did.

I had to settle some issues with the kid who made fun of the holes in my shoes. Mom did take me to the secondhand store and got me a pair of shoes that did not have holes in them. One day after school, I was following this kid that made fun of the holes in my shoes. He saw me, and I could tell that he was anxious. He started running. He was no match for me. We were off school grounds. I tackled him and started hitting him in his face and nose with my fist. I shoved his head into the ground. He started bleeding from his mouth and nose. I rubbed his face in the grass and dirt. I grabbed both his arms and pulled them behind him as hard as I could. As he turned over, I kicked him in his balls.

The next day, he and his mother were talking with Ms. Eggleston. I was called over and asked if I did all of this. The kid looked horrible. I said, "Yes, and it was off school grounds." I told his mom if he continues to make fun of me, it will happen again. I told his mother to tell her son to stay away from me and nothing more would happen. I told Ms. Eggleston that she was not going to paddle me because this was off school grounds. I told Ms. Eggleston, "I know you are very disappointed because you are not going to paddle me." Furthermore, at this time, she did not have a paddle. I wonder where it went.

In the tenth grade, I made the sports page every game. People loved to see me play in basketball and baseball. We were first in the conference in basketball and baseball mainly because of me. I made first team all-conference as well as first team all-district in both baseball and basketball. I was looking forward to the eleventh grade. We were projected to be number one in the conference in basketball and baseball mainly because of me. After the first three to four games, I was scoring 4 to 6 points. The year before, it would have been 25–30 points per game. Nobody on the team could score like me. We had lost the first five games. Nobody was passing me the ball. Everybody was wondering why. The reason was jealousy among all the players on the team, the superintendent, the principal, the school board, and some teachers. The superintendent's son was one of the players. It was a terrible year for me. Before too long, there was a town known for its basketball and baseball programs as well as good academics that wanted us to move there. They offered Mom and Dad several things if we would move there. There were eventually three other towns that also spoke with Dad and offered a package of incentives if we would move there. After practicing with the first school four times, I was convinced that was where I wanted to go. I felt that we would have an incredible team. I liked the boys on the team. They welcomed me with open arms. They were going to be good in baseball also. The coach was excellent, and he felt we had an excellent chance to win the state.

When Dad told me we could not move, I was devastated. I was numb and so saddened I began to cry. I knew I could not change Dad's mind. If only he knew how I felt. I did not care about playing sports or going to Salina schools. Instead of us being first in the conference, we were last. We had lost all ten games badly. The same for baseball.

I did hit a home run to propel us to the playoffs. We lost the first game. Over the summer, I tried to forget what happened to me in the eleventh grade. I was just not into sports or school. The enthusiasm for sports just was not there. I really felt I should have quit sports midway through basketball. I was just not into sports or school. I did not play any sports for about three weeks. It would have been best for all parties involved.

About midway throughout the summer, the desire for competitive sports increased, as well as during half of the basketball season. Unfortunately, I was injured during the first football game as well as during the first basketball game. I missed the entire football season and half of the basketball season. The basketball team did not win a game until I came back. We won the very first game when I came back. I wonder what would have happened to me if we had all played together my junior year. I wonder what would have happened if we had moved to this other town that was projected to win the state. All of the above will never be known because of unprecedented jealousy emanating from the players, my counselor, the superintendent, the principal, and the school board. Even though the superintendent had a son on the basketball team, I did not think the superintendent would do something like this. I thought he was a better person than what he displayed. I think I was disliked by my counselor, principal, and superintendent because I did not enroll at Northeastern, a teacher's college in Oklahoma. I think they were all disgusted with me.

Again, my counselor, Mr. Thompson, told me that nobody coming from Salina public schools had ever graduated from Oklahoma State University (OSU) or the University of Oklahoma (OU). Furthermore, my counselor told me to change my major to something other than premed. I told Mr. Thompson I was not going to enroll at Northeastern and I was not going to change my major, end of discussion. When I graduated from Oklahoma State University with a grade point average of 3.8, while taking the most difficult courses that Oklahoma State had to offer, I told my counselor, the superintendent, and the principal. I did the same thing when I graduated from medical school. I made sure they knew they were wrong trying to push me into a major I did not want and trying to enroll me in a college I did not want too. "Shame on you three. Furthermore, you three were trying to jeopardize my enrollment at Oklahoma State University. Shame on you." I was so glad when high school was over. I had to have knee surgery again. This was done one week before college started. I was discharged on a Sunday and put everything that I needed into Roger's car; and I, Roger, and Mom went to start me to college. I stayed off campus in a one-room apartment that had a closet, a desk, and a bed. This was at a relatively large house that was owned by a very nice older lady who also cooked incredible meals. I stayed there for two years. I started college on crutches. They were a major impediment. I did not miss any classes, and I carried some books in my briefcase.

Bob Piguet helped me a lot. He met me at my last class, which was a long way from my apartment. It would have taken me probably an hour to get to my apartment if I had to walk on crutches.

Reasons for writing my autobiography:

1. To present information regarding our ancestors. Hopefully, this will be informative to generations to come.

2. To try to depict how hard it was growing up in poverty and in an impoverished small town in Oklahoma. I knew that there had to be something better in life.

3. To show how my counselor and the principal tried to jeopardize my enrollment at Oklahoma State University. With my poor education at Salina public schools, what were the chances of me

becoming a physician? There was a lot of doubt that I could do this.

4. Your dreams. Never give up on your dreams even in the face of a major adversity. I did not give up, and my dreams came true.

When we were vacationing in Captiva, Florida, Sissy and I would sit Mom down and ask her questions for a couple of hours. Mom seemed to enjoy this. We got a lot of information from her. We did this two times a year for about five years.

I wrote this autobiography for several reasons. My Wife and cousin Lige frequently discuss ancestry. There are many more unanswered questions in comparison with factual information about my ancestry. Dad's mother stated that she could trace our ancestry back to George Washington. She died before anyone could sit down with her to have her demonstrate this. This is what happened so many times. Following our ancestry is given very low priority, shoved under the rug, not to be thought about until somebody dies. The majority of the information in my autobiography is not known by my family. The majority of the information comes from me and my mother. I wanted to capture the past and to write about the good and bad situations that made up my life experiences. I wanted to tell about the people, both good and bad, who passed through my life. I tried to give a description both mentally and physically of these individuals. I want my family to know how hard it was to grow up in poverty as well as Salina. I have tried to depict how different my childhood was in comparison with that of my children growing up.

An example of the level of poverty that we lived in was that we never really knew what it was like to have the "necessities" for living. The only necessity we had was electricity. If I took a bath, it was behind the potbellied stove with soap, water, and a small basin. This was the only place to take a bath in winter; otherwise it would be too cold (Sissy's story in poverty). In writing this autobiography, I also wanted to touch on "following your dreams." Do not let people get in your way.

I had several people telling me not to enroll in premed and not to go to Oklahoma State University. When I graduated from medical school, I let everyone know that my dream was accomplished, and "shame on them for discouraging me." I have tried to describe my education in Salina public schools. I think very few people thought my dream could be accomplished, especially with my education in Salina. I went into premed at OSU with a lot of doubt about my ability to "make it." Perhaps the reason no one from Salina public schools graduated from OSU or OU was that the education they received in Salina public schools was so poor.

Volume I of this book will cover my birth up to my graduation from high school, 1949–1967. Volume II will cover my stay at Oklahoma State University until graduation in four years, 1967–1971; my stay at Wake Forest Medical School until my graduation in four years, 1971–1975; my stay at Northwestern University Hospital for internship and residency in Chicago, Illinois, until graduation in three years, 1975–1978; and my stay at Vanderbilt University Medical Center in Gastroenterology in Nashville, Tennessee, until graduation, 1978–1980. Volume III will cover 1980–present.

CHAPTER 1

Idabell—My Mom

Mom was born November 18, 1920. She was born on an 80-acre farm. She attended grade school at COLE District a country School through the 8th grade. She attended high school at Pryor Oklahoma, graduating in 1938. Both Mom and Dad lived through the depression. Mom and Dad got married October 24, 1942, in Claremore Oklahoma. Mom worked as a store clerk at different stores most of her life. She retired in 1985.

Mom was an angelic person. She was born and raised on an eighty-acre farm in Oklahoma. Mother actually enjoyed living on the farm. The only outside food staples they needed were flour, sugar, and coffee. Mom described her mother as a very businesslike individual.

Mom did not care for her dad. She would frequently ask her mother why she had married her dad. Mom's mother, Mary Jane, lived in a situation where Mary Jane's stepmother was very mean to her. Marriage was the only way out of this situation. Mary Jane was fifteen years old when she married him. Mary Jane's maiden name was Mary Jane Scroggins, an Indian name. Her husband had been married before and had four living children. His first wife had died from cancer. Mary Jane and her husband had six children; only two survived to adulthood: Idabell and her sister, Lillie Mae Morton.

Mom described the following situation. It was April 27, 1942, around 5:00 p.m. when Mom and Grandma were in their orchard picking apples. Mom stated that there was a foreboding, eerie stillness with no wind at all. Mom described numerous black clouds everywhere.

She told her mom "…something bad was happening." They hurriedly picked up the remaining apples and went into the cellar. Lillie Mae was ahead in the cellar. They stayed in the cellar for a couple of hours. Just as Mom and Grandma entered the cellar, heavy wind and rain commenced. When they exited the cellar, the sun was shining and from what they could tell (because they had no TV, radio, or paper to get information from), there was no damage to the house and barns.

The eighty-acre farm we were living on was self-serving. There were thirty head of cattle. My grandmother, Mary Scroggins (maiden name), sold cream and butter. There was no electricity in the house; therefore, the milk was no good after about twenty-four hours.

The extra milk was given to the dog and pigs. The cellar was the coolest place to go to hold the milk for twenty-four hours. The cellar was kept very well. There was a lot of canned food in the cellar also. If Mary needed to have extra money, she would sell a cow. Her cows were excellent dairy cows.

During very hot days, with high humidity, Mom would take me and Sissy to the cellar, where it was cooler. Because of this, they moved a rocking chair and a crib to the cellar. Mom would rock me; Sissy would be in the crib. Momma had a fan with a picture of Jesus. Retreating to the cellar and using the fan helped a lot. I would go to sleep in the arms of my mother. My diet consisted mainly of unpasteurized milk. There was also an excellent orchard and garden on the farm. Because the farmhouse had no electricity, coal oil lamps were used to light up the house. This, unfortunately, increased the temperature in the house to unbearable levels. I remember as a young boy sleeping on the screened porch and hearing the coyotes howling all night long. There could have been wolves also. The name of the creek was Wolf Creek.

This time in my life, after we had moved back to Salina, Mom would contact this man whom she called Wild Bill, because he drove like a maniac. Grandma enjoyed us being around her. She was always talking about everything; we certainly enjoyed Grandma also. She would usually feed us chicken or ham plus the usual two to three veggies that would come from the garden. Grandma always had an excellent garden. Grandma had a lot of chickens. The chickens were free to roam because they liked to scratch the grass. Her yard was mostly dirt; therefore, Grandma did not have to depend on someone cutting the grass. When we went to Grandma's house, generally speaking, Grandma would tell Lillie Mae to go and get a chicken to kill and eat. I called this "chicken on the hoof." I remember being so hungry that I could not get enough to eat. Mom would tell me to stop eating so much. Grandma would say, "Just let him eat all he wants. He is a growing boy." I therefore ate all I wanted. And to top it off, we usually had a cherry cobbler or peach cobbler.

We went to see Grandma two to three times per month while school was out. It was always fun to play with Lige. Grandma had an old barn that we were not supposed to go to. It was a very unstable barn. Inevitably, we made our way to the loft of the barn. It is amazing we did not encounter snakes in the loft of the barn. It is also amazing that we did not fall from the loft. There were rats and mice, which we could see, but we never got bit.

Pigs were kept in the bottom of the barn. Eventually, there were long telephone poles put up to help stabilize the barn. Unfortunately, at some point there was a storm with high winds that blew the barn down. Luckily, the livestock were all saved. We had to put up a fence around a fairly large area to keep the pigs in. They loved to have milk on a daily basis and sometimes were fed milk twice a day.

CHAPTER 3

Poverty

The definition of poverty is "not having enough material possessions or income for a person or family's needs." We did not have a refrigerator, oven, phone, TV, automobile, air conditioner, indoor washer/dryer, toilet, and running hot water. We had a very small house with four rooms. One bedroom was unheated in the wintertime; only one room was heated, which was poorly heated by a potbellied stove. My bed was on the floor close to the stove. We had inadequate income when Daddy was laid off, that is, $25 a month. Layoffs usually happened three to four times per year. This was mostly when Republicans were in power. That is why Mom and Dad always voted for the Democrats.

Mom did not realize that the Democratic Party during those times is the Republican Party now. Mom hated it when we talked about politics; therefore, we seldom "went there." In 1949, the town of Salina was certainly an impoverished town. Most people were on welfare. Salina is where the Cherokee Indians settled when President Jackson drove them from North Carolina. This was called the Trail of Tears; many of the Indians died.

I had to be delivered at Grandma's house because there was just no money. Shortly after I was delivered, Mom put me in my crib. She went to the kitchen, and before too long, Mom heard me crying. She knew this cry was different from my usual cry. She hurriedly came to the bedroom where I was. Much to her surprise, there was a huge rat chewing on my right hand. Blood was everywhere. She was unable to kill the rat. Mom took me to the kitchen where she poured water over my hand. She found a very large area on my right thumb where the rat had been chewing. It had chewed to the bone. She put a bandage on the area. It is a wonder that I did not get an infection. Grandma and Mom could not give Dr. Meyer, the family physician who delivered me, any money. Instead, Grandma gave him eggs, milk, butter, and cream. Dr. Meyer knew this was excellent food. He went to his home and put it in his refrigerator.

Before I was born, Dad had to go to California to work on an orchard picking oranges. There were no jobs in the Salina/Pryor area. After we moved to California to be with Dad, we lived in a very small house on the orchard, where families lived while the fathers worked picking oranges on the orchard. We lived there for two years. Mom and Dad did not want to live in California. They saved as much money as they could.

When they came back to Oklahoma, they rented a house in Salina. Dad got a job with Mr. Childress doing odd jobs around town. He also got a job making awnings. Mom loved this little white house despite all the missing amenities as depicted above. We did have electricity. The rent was $4 per month. Dad finally got a job at McDonnell Douglas. A coworker of his from Spavinaw picked Dad up every day. They worked in the same department. Money was good except when they had layoffs.

Mom washed our clothes on a scrubboard. Eventually, she met a lady at church who would come and get us to take us to her laundromat. I remember Mom putting me on one of these washers so I could play with my cars and trucks. The laundromat wastewater emptied right into the river. What an environmental disaster.

We never accepted rations from the welfare department; Lillie Mae did. This was a good thing because Lillie Mae could not take care of a big garden by herself. Lillie Mae would give me the white beans because she said they caused her abdominal pain.

Eventually, Mom got a job working at Mr. McClay's grocery store. This helped a lot. She was working for $3 a day, plus we got discounts on our groceries. I would frequently go and get bones and scraps for the dogs outside the grocery store. The dogs waited because people who were leaving the grocery store would feed them. They were stray dogs but in a much better shape than the typical stray dog that I rehabbed. I will never forget, as a small boy, walking by the meat counter seeing a weenie in the counter. It looked incredibly good. Mom saw me leaning up against the window to the icebox staring at the weenie. Mom took me by the hand and pulled me away from the counter. Mom told me, "Sonny, we could not afford the weenie." At age seventy, I can still see that weenie in the meat counter. I don't know who bought it, but whoever did had an incredible treat.

Dad had to go every month to sign up so we could get the $25 a month. I went several times with Dad. There was bus service to Pryor in the morning and bus service back to Salina in the afternoon. We had to buy a ticket at the drugstore. There was a terribly dangerous bridge over Grand River, with only one-way traffic at a time. The bottom of the bridge was loose wooden planks. If the water was low in the river, from the bus, we could frequently see the huge eighty- to one-hundred-pound catfish swimming. (These were the fish that Jeff Dobbs liked. He could gig them with a large fork. From the large catfish, Jeff Dobbs would make what he called catfish steaks. People in the Salina/Pryor area loved these steaks. He would sell out in a very short time.) Going over the bridge with the bus, we could hear worrisome sounds from the bridge itself. If there had been a collapse disaster, it would spell death to a lot of people. I doubt if there were very many people who could swim riding the bus. I could not swim at that particular time. I never saw my father swim, although I was told that he was a very good swimmer.

One to two times per month, Mom would go to see her mother. Sissy and I loved to go and see Grandma, Lillie Mae, and Lige. There was a wild man, described by his driving habits, whom Mom would call to take us to Grandma's house and to bring us back to our house in the afternoon. He was the only person who took us to Grandma's house.

When we would go to Grandma's house, Grandma would tell Lillie Mae to go out and get a chicken and kill it. We would have the chicken for lunch. There was also a lot of good food from the garden. Mom always helped Lillie Mae. From the big garden, we would have potatoes, salad, and beans. There was usually cherry cobbler also made. Oh! Was this ever so good. Mom would tell me not to eat so much. Grandma would tell Mom to leave me alone and let me eat. Sissy and I looked forward to playing with Lige.

Mom, Sissy, and I would go to Pryor one to two times a year. This was for clothes and shoes. We usually got one to two pairs of shoes a year. If we needed more, we would go to the secondhand store in Salina. Usually on a Saturday morning, Dad would walk from one end of the house to the other talking to Mom, who was in the kitchen, about getting rich by raising chickens and selling their eggs. Sissy would be on the floor playing jacks. Dad would give me two to three cans of Prince Albert tobacco for me to roll him 125–150 cigarettes. I would begin to feel the effects of the tobacco after about 75 cigarettes.

We would receive a Sears, Montgomery Ward, and Aldens catalog just before Christmas. There were no stores in Salina that sold more than food. There were minimal items other than food sold in Pryor. Therefore, Sissy and I picked out what we wanted for Christmas from these catalogs. Sears was the best to pick from. When it was time for these catalogs to come, we would run home to look at the catalogs to pick out what we wanted for Christmas. As mentioned above, this is how we got our toys for Christmas. What we ordered would come to the post office or to our home. For some reason, Christmas was always good to Sissy and me. I think this emanated from Mom not being able to decorate and celebrate Christmas because her dad felt that decorating was too commercial; therefore, her dad would not allow her to decorate or have a Christmas tree. We also always enjoyed looking for toys at the dump. When we went walking in the woods, at the entrance to the trails, there was a big dump where Sissy and I would look for toys. We frequently found toys that we could play with. When we had a friend walking in the woods with us, we would not look for toys because we did not want our friends to know we got toys from the dump.

Grandma did not have any of the amenities in her house either. She did not even have electricity like we did. She had old-fashioned lanterns, which burned coal oil. In the summertime, when it was very hot, the lamps made things even worse because the lamps put out a lot of heat.

I hated living in poverty. I saw what the other kids had, and I would wonder why we did not have these things. I don't know why Dad thought our living conditions were adequate. Why he quit school in the tenth grade, I don't know. Why Mom or Dad did not drive a car, I don't know. Dad could have graduated from high school and gone to Northeastern and gotten a degree in something. That something could have been in teaching or accounting. He did go to a small college in Chillicothe, Missouri, where he graduated first in his class in accounting. Daddy was no dummy. He did not use his intelligence to better himself. Furthermore, why Mom and Dad settled in the town of Salina, I do not know. Salina had absolutely nothing to offer Mom or Dad. He could have had a decent job in accounting but not in Salina. Pryor had more to offer than Salina.

Why they settled in Salina is beyond comprehension. I know that Mom loved the little white house on the corner where we lived. She loved the location across the street from the church, one block from Main Street, where the stores were and where she had a job, one block from high school. I never asked Mom why she was satisfied living without all the amenities as noted above. Most people had at least some of these amenities. I would go to grade school and listen to all of the kids talking about what they had seen on TV the night before. I could do nothing but walk away and wonder about how nice it would be to have a TV.

I was in high school when Roger Klinger bought Mom and Dad their TV. When Dad got home from work, he would sit in his favorite chair and Mom would feed him from the TV tray. He would watch TV until around 10:00 p.m. when Mom was done cleaning in the kitchen. When she was done in the kitchen, Mom would join Dad watching TV. By this time, Sissy and I were doing other things. I was about fourteen when Dad decided to put in an indoor toilet and a hot water heater. When Sissy graduated from high school, we got a phone. Thank goodness we could stop going to Main Street to use the nasty pay phone.

Dad bought forty acres about six miles from Salina. He really bought this "dirt cheap" from Sylvia, one of his half sisters. Mom and Dad moved all of the items from the other bedroom up to the attic. This could be done after a floor was put into the attic. With all of these things being done, we thought we were moving up to join the "elite" people. I still slept on the floor or the couch. When Sissy was away at school, I got the bedroom.

It is hard to say what effect being born and raised in poverty had on me. Like Mom told Ms. Bunnel years ago, I had to go to college. I too knew that I had to go to college and move away from Salina. Why Dad did not know this for himself, I do not know. We never discussed this.

Dad and I never discussed sensitive questions about our poverty. Questions like this, Dad would not give a good explanation anyway. I think I am a better person for having been born and raised in poverty and working my way out of it. It has given me fortitude throughout my life. I can truly say I lived it.

CHAPTER 4

Dad

Dad's name is unknown to us. It is possible that the G. W. stands for George Washington. There are some census records from that time recording the name George. Kinfolk on Dad's side stated that they could trace our ancestors back to George Washington. Dad was born to Oscar and Ruby Yarborough. He also had a younger sister named Ann. Oscar and Ruby divorced after approximately five years of marriage.

Dad was born on July 5, 1917 and died May 20, 1977. He lived in a tent on Grand River with his stepdad and mother. His stepdad Jeff was a fisherman. He sold a lot of fish, especially catfish in the Salina, Pryor area. Dad, while growing up, worked on a farm picking cotton and helping his stepdad picking cotton.

Dad went to Salina school. He played baseball and basketball. People who knew him said he was an excellent athlete. Dad went to the tenth grade and quit school. I am sure that Ruby or Oscar had nothing to do with Dad or Ann's academic or athletic endeavors. Apparently, Ann was also a very good basketball player.

I was getting ready for Oscar's funeral. I had missed one day of school, and I was going to miss another. Sharon Halloway was at the front door with a few other girls. I went to the front door, and before I could say anything, Sharon said, "Gosh, you are good-looking." She wanted to know if I was going to be in school.

I told her, "Not today, but I will be there tomorrow." She and her friends were happy about this. I thanked her for her compliment.

Dad attended grade school through the 8th grade at Centerhill Oklahoma Country School. He then went to Salina High School and quit after the 10th grade. Rather than finishing high school he went to a business school in Chillicothe Missouri, graduating number one in his class. Unfortunately, due to economic conditions at that time, he was unable to use his accounting degree.

He therefore moved to live on a ten-acre farm. He bought cows, pigs, chickens, and made a big garden. From this, he sold eggs, milk, and produce from the farm. Rent on the farm was $8.00 a month.

Dad did a lot of roaming. He would hop the train going north and do some work in a couple of towns up north. There were no jobs in Salina or Pryor. Dad was a very good swimmer. Mom could not swim at all. Mom's motto was "If you stay away from the water, you don't need to know how to swim." In those days, there were no programs to teach kids how to swim.(All my kids with my wife have taken swimming lessons and know how to swim. I learned how to swim at a baseball camp. Over a year period of time, I developed into a very good swimmer. Jeff had something to do with the draft. He got paid very much for doing this. Generally, the train would stop in Salina, although occasionally, it did not stop. Dad had to jump on and off of the train while it was moving. One time he jumped into a large tree stump. He suffered a large laceration on his leg and a knee injury. His mom treated him with kerosene and charcoal. He did go to see Dr. Cameron in Pryor. He was given penicillin, the wonder drug. Occasionally, when we were young, Dad would show us the wound scar. It was black from the charcoal. Dad would occasionally develop swelling of his knee with stiffness. I am sure he had what's called "internal derangement syndrome" of his knee. He never went to see an orthopedic doctor. He never missed a day of work. Jeff, his stepdad, declared GW unfit for the army or Marines because of his infection and because of what I believe to be the internal derangement of his knee. Ruby married Jeff and had six children. There were five girls and one boy. Dad and Ann had a lot to do with caring for these six children. None of Dad's half siblings went to college. Jeff was a captain in the Marines. Jeff told us a story of his time in the Marines. He was out on patrol and came upon this fairly large tunnel. He needed to make sure it was clear. As he was going farther into the tunnel, he could see that there was a Vietnamese person in the tunnel. Neither one did anything other than stare at each other. Neither one attempted to kill the other, and Jeff slowly backed out of the tunnel.

At about age fourteen, Dad became interested in a girl, my mom, Idabell. Before too long, they fell in love. Dad would paddle a boat across Grand River, up Wolf Creek to the bridge. There was a very busy gravel road running over Wolf Creek. The eighty-acre farm that Mom's family lived on bordered Wolf Creek; there was also ten acres across Wolf Creek that was very good soil. Mom would walk down the gravel road to meet Dad. Mom usually brought a picnic. Dad would usually be waiting for Mom. Dad would usually help Mom with the chores. There were no telephones or electricity, so Mom and Dad had to make their plans two to three days in advance to see each other. Dad usually carried a shotgun with him. Around Wolf Creek, you had to be very careful about the snakes.

Although Dad did not graduate from high school, he was a very brilliant person. He did go to Chillicothe, Missouri, graduating number one in his class. He studied accounting at Chillicothe. Unfortunately, he never used his degree. He could have gotten a lot of money and help if he had followed through with the degree. I am sure he did not pursue this further because my mother did not want to move. After Mom's graduation from Pryor High School, they decided to get married. They went to the justice of the peace in Claremore to get married. They rented a house in Salina for $4 a month. Dad cut wood for $3 per rick or face cord. The work was backbreaking. He was told by family in California that he could get a fairly good job in the orchards picking fruit. He had no choice but to go to California. He was hired, and the money was very good. Dad was sending money back home. They were all very kind to Dad. They knew how much Dad and Ann cared for them as youngsters. While in California, he lived in welfare housing, meaning very small houses with two to three rooms. It was a small three-room house. After about eighteen months apart, when I was fourteen months old, Mom decided to move to California. Mom, Sissy, and I all took a train to Ventura, California. This was the first time Dad saw me. Sissy and I played well together. All of his half sisters wanted to take care of me and Sissy to give Mom a break. Mom was afraid that someone would steal us; furthermore, she had nothing to do anyway. I think she very much liked to be around us anyway. We were in California for about two years. When it got cold in the orchard, the burners were lit to try to raise the temperature. The burners burned coal oil. The next morning, Sissy and I had a black substance around our noses and mouths.

Almost every Saturday, the following regimen was followed, almost, to a tee. Early in the morning, I was given two cans of Prince Albert to roll cigarettes for Daddy. I got very good rolling cigarettes. I would roll 135–150 cigarettes; after about 75, I could feel the effects of the tobacco. Sissy would be on the floor playing jacks, and Dad would walk from the front door to the back door smoking cigarettes and chewing Red Man tobacco, talking about getting rich selling eggs. Nobody could tell Daddy anything. We all knew Dad was bloviating. Mom would reply incessantly, "Now, shuggy, all of that is up to you." He would usually pace and talk until about noon when he would take his rolled cigarettes and put them in another can. At that time, I could go shooting hoops. Before too long, there would be somebody that would come and play horse with me. I was unbeatable with my new hoop. I will never forget when I first connected with a jump shot. I was working on this for a long time. It took quite some time in order to do the shot. I will never forget me running to the living room where Daddy would be sitting next to the radio listening to the University of Oklahoma football. I told Dad about my jump shot. He did not seem all that surprised. He just said to continue to practice.

After the University of Oklahoma football game, we would divide kids into about four teams. This got to be an incredible affair that the children loved to take aim with. Each team had to have the same number of females since they were not athletically inclined most of the time. We had to allow some good teams to lose to make things a little more equal. Mom fixed hamburgers, ice cream, and coleslaw for us to eat. The game had to end around eight thirty to eight forty-five because the *Grand Ole Opry* was on. Sissy never liked the *Grand Ole Opry*. She would play jacks with her friends until bedtime. At the beginning of the *Grand Ole Opry*, in the summertime, all the shades were open and the door was open with the lights off. The lights had to be off every time that the *Grand Ole Opry* was on. Why Daddy wanted this done like this, I have no idea. In the wintertime, the shades were closed, as well as the door. Like a dairy cow knowing which stall is hers: I, Mom, and Dad knew which stalls we had. I would be on one end of the couch, Mom would be in the middle, and Dad would be on the other end of the couch. Mom would be rubbing Dad's head and back all the way through the *Grand Ole Opry*. Halfway through the show, Dad would be dozing off. I would occasionally rub Mom's head and neck, and she would also start to doze off halfway through the show. I did not have anybody to rub my neck and head, but I would still get tired. Mom loved Minnie Pearl. Mom would occasionally get into the music, and she would tap her feet and wave her hands like a conductor. We were a hopeless trio. When Dad smoked cigarettes during the *Grand Ole Opry*, he would frequently blow smoke rings in the dark. He was very good at doing this. Dad would frequently order fifteen to twenty baby chicks, and half of those would be for us to eat, the other half for laying eggs and so on.

Dad never brushed his teeth. I do not know why he didn't brush his teeth. I just wonder if this was not prevalent with his sister or any of the half sisters or half brother. He therefore developed pain from the cavities. He would use Merthiolate. There were very small cotton swabs that one would dip into the Merthiolate and then put the swab into the area where the pain was coming from. Like I said before, I had no idea why he didn't brush his teeth.

After about two years of living in California, Mom and Dad were getting lonesome for the people in Oklahoma. When Mom and Dad moved back, they rented a house in Salina for $4 a month. Mom and Dad did not have an automobile. Dad was hired by Mr. Childress doing odd jobs around Salina. They were renting the house from Mr. Childress.

While Daddy was working for Mr. Childress, he wanted to get in with McDonnell Douglas in Tulsa, Oklahoma. They paid an excellent salary as well as good benefits. When we moved back to Oklahoma, Dad got a job with McDonnell Douglas. Dad would frequently cash his check and bring home rolls of dimes, quarters, etc. Many of these silver coins are in a lock box in Pryor. We also have two lock boxes that are here in Mequon, Wisconsin.

If a person was not working and unemployed, money was $25 a month. This is what we had to live on. The problem was getting Dad to Tulsa because he did not have an automobile and a license to drive. Why he never drove, I have no idea. Came to find out there was a man from Spavinaw, a small town approximately twenty minutes from Salina, that Dad could get a ride with. Six months later, things were going just fine. The gentleman from Spavinaw and Dad worked in the same department at McDonnell Douglas as craters/packers. If there was a McDonnell Douglas airplane that needed some parts, they had to build a wooden frame for the part to be shipped in to anywhere in the world. Sometimes they all had to work overtime. The money was excellent when this was the case. Dad liked the job very much.(I will never forget that Ed from our family; he and his father took us to Spavinaw for fishing. We caught probably fifty perch. Sissy and I were baptized shortly before going fishing. It was an incredible day all the way around.) There was also good fishing in Wolf Creek. Dad usually carried a shotgun with him. The area around Wolf Creek one had to be very careful because of snakes.

Dad never actively socialized with anybody outside of his immediate family. The number of acquaintances he had could be counted on one hand. I would not say any of these were true friends.

Gunnar was what we called then a mentally retarded man, about six feet five, who would come to see Dad about one time a month. He lived in a two-room shack with a well and outdoor toilet. I don't know how he cleaned himself. In the summertime, he had bad body odor. When he sat in our chairs, there would be the smell of stool. Sissy and I would check this out when he would leave after he visited with Dad for one to two hours. The chair would have the strong smell of stool when he left. Many times, the seat would have to be washed before it could be used again. Gunnar always carried a single-shot 12-gauge shotgun with him everywhere he went. Frequently, people would mock and tease him because of his mental retardation. I never saw him in anything other than overalls. Dad was probably his only friend. Gunnar would go with us when we went walking in the woods. He frequently went fishing in Grand River. He loved catfish.

In wintertime, the only place that was warm in the entire house was very close to the potbelly stove. We, therefore, had two chairs on opposite sides of the stove. Sissy and I would be in a corner of the room with our coats on playing jacks. If someone came to see Dad, they would have to sit in one of the chairs close to the stove. They could not see each other; they could only hear each other talk.

Another acquaintance of Dad was Bill Brewer. He would come to see Dad about the same frequency as Gunnar. Bill was a short individual who walked dragging his right leg, and he had a slight impairment in his right arm. Bill had a history of tertiary syphilis. He had a slight speech impediment too. After our house was burglarized, he was the individual who told the police that he saw a black car parked out front with a man with a hat on standing in the front yard. He was going to the store for groceries. On his way back home, which was about forty-five minutes later, the man and the black car were gone. Bill was even implicated as the individual who burglarized our house. I highly doubt this because I doubt if Bill even knew that Dad even had a metal box with money in it, which was kept under the bed. I doubt if Dad would have shown Bill the metal box and told him where he kept it.

Mr. Hill was my shop and science teacher that lived one block away from us. He was an excellent, caring teacher. He loved coming over and talking with Dad. He thought Dad was a very brilliant individual, and so he was. Here you had one individual who stopped schooling when he was in tenth grade (Dad), talking about rockets landing a man on the moon, math, medicine, woodworking, etc. with a man who taught about these subjects. All these individuals were smokers. They would easily smoke one to two packs of Winston cigarettes while talking. The smoke would be very heavy throughout the living room and kitchen. They would usually visit one to two hours, but if a topic was very interesting, the conversation could last two and a half to three hours. I would hear about all of this at school. Mr. Hill and his wife had two girls. He loved to watch me play basketball and baseball. As of this writing, Mr. Hill was still living. I think he developed emphysema later in life.

Another acquaintance that came over to see Dad was Mrs. Cox. She lived across the street from us. She usually came while we were in church on a Sunday. I guess because Dad was the only person home. She, too, smoked. When we came home from church, the living room had so much smoke in it—it almost impaired our vision. She would usually leave around fifteen to twenty minutes after we got home. She was a very nice lady. She and Mr. Cox had a daughter by the name of Sally Cox. She was my teacher in the seventh and eighth grade. She taught me science and math. She was an excellent teacher. Mrs. Cox lived to be about 105 years old. She maintained her faculties until her death.

I never knew Dad to actively go to somebody else's house to visit. I never saw Dad in a church, except when Sissy got married, I got married, and Dad's funeral.

Dad loved to read about science, medicine, math, rockets, and the universe. I think he would have absolutely loved a computer and the iPhone. If Dad had taken care of the melanoma earlier, then he and Mom could have enjoyed an iPhone and computer together. When I bought Mom the iPhone, she did not have anybody to teach her how to use it. I tried to help her as much as I could over the phone. About three weeks before I had planned a trip to Oklahoma, Mom had a stroke and did not recover. I had planned to teach her about her iPhone every day.

I am sure Mom, Dad, and Sissy are all in heaven enjoying one another's fellowship.

CHAPTER 5

Sissy

Sissy was fourteen months older than me. She was delivered in a hospital in Pryor, Oklahoma. Her growth and development was normal. Sissy did have asthma. She had acute exacerbation of asthma as manifested by shortness of breath, cough, and wheezing. She was on a medicine on a daily basis. There were certain things that would precipitate shortness of breath, such as cats, horses, cows, playing hard, running a lot, and so on; all manifested problems with asthma. If the shortness of breath and coughing and wheezing did not resolve quickly with the inhalers, she would have to go and get an injection of epinephrine from Dr. Meyer. As time went on, she got better as her tolerance increased to all of the above situations. When we all got older, I was able to play with Sissy without an acute exacerbation of her asthma. I remember Sissy making pies out of dirt and mud. She wanted me to eat them. We played in the yard under the watchful eye of Mom. She was always concerned that somebody would kidnap us.

One day, Sissy made some dirt pies, which I ate a lot of. I had dirt all over my face. Mom wanted to know why I had all of this dirt on my face. I told Mom Sissy made me some dirt pies, which I had to eat. Mom grabbed me by the hand and took me to where Sissy was. She told both of us that Sissy better not make these pies for Sonny to eat. She asked if that was understood. She stated that it was okay to play in the dirt, "but you better not eat it anymore." Playing in the dirt was fun. I had small cars, big and small trucks, so I could move dirt here and there. I also had a bulldozer, trucks, and small people. The opposite side of the garden was where we had a row of trees that we could climb. The opposite side of the garden was where we played in the dirt.

Sissy could climb those trees with ease. I would watch her climb, and I would use the same limbs as she did. I would climb high into the tree. Not only would Sissy climb the tree with ease, but also she could come down with ease. There I was, high up in the tree, and I could not come back down. I would begin to cry. Mom could climb a couple of limbs and would usually tell me the limbs to stand on so that I could come back down. One good thing, I never fell from climbing a tree. As I got older, I was able to climb the trees with ease. The side and back of the house was where the tent would get put up. I got my badge given to me by Smokey Bear. He wanted me to watch for forest fires. I climbed the trees and put up strings of telephone wire so that if I did find a fire, I could call Smokey. I was about eight years old at this time.

Every day around one o'clock, we had to take a nap for about an hour. The reason was that Mom had heard that doing this would help prevent polio. There frequently would be somebody coming onto the porch and wanting us to come out and play. We had to be asleep for a while, usually about an hour, before we went back out and played. Usually, the person on the porch would be either Robert McDonald or Bobby Baldridgee. If Bobby wanted to play a sport such as kicking a football, or throwing a baseball, Robert would go home because he was not an athlete. His father never really gave him the ability to play baseball or football or basketball. When we got through with our nap, we were free to go out and play with other individuals. I would usually go to the basketball hoop and shoot baskets rather than do what Sissy and her friends were doing.

I remember standing in line to get the polio vaccine. It did not matter whether it was cowboys/Indians or a sport; Sissy could hold her own. Sissy had to be careful playing hard, especially with running, because she would develop wheezing, which would usually go away with her inhalers. Generally speaking, her shortness of breath and wheezing would resolve with the inhalers very rapidly. If it did not resolve and the wheezing got worse, she then would have to go to Dr. Meyer's office for an epinephrine injection. It, generally speaking, resolved her symptoms rather rapidly. The wheezing and shortness of breath got better as Sissy got older. She hardly had to have an epinephrine injection. She would use the inhaler as the main medication. Sissy could not do very strenuous farmwork because it would exacerbate her asthma. Like I said before, she was getting markedly better, which was an incredible gift. Sissy, in high school, was able to play basketball without a problem. Sissy was guard on the high school team. In high school, Sissy was friends with several kids. She was especially close to Sharon Ingersoll and Sharon Alberty. Sharon Alberty would come to our house quite frequently, especially on a game day for basketball. On days when there was no basketball, Sharon Alberty would come to our house to be picked up by her dad. We would be playing basketball in the backyard when the men from the telephone office would come over around four thirty. They loved to come over and play basketball with us. We certainly had enough people to play with five players on two teams. Sharon had an operative procedure because of her abdominal pain. She was admitted to the hospital in Pryor because of an overwhelming infection called sepsis. The infection was overwhelming, and Sharon died from this infection. Sissy really took this bad. Sissy and Sharon Ingersoll enrolled at Northeastern College after high school. Sissy wanted to go into speech pathology.

Sharon Ingersoll went out on a date with a guy she met when she was a freshman at Northeastern. They were in a park with the motor running. They became asphyxiated. They were found dead the next day. Sissy took this very hard again.

Shortly after this, there were three boys going to Oklahoma State that were coming home to Salina when they decided to pass a car in a no-pass zone, resulting in a head-on collision. All three boys were killed. One of the boys was Ms. Jetton's son. Ms. Jetton's son was enrolled in engineering. He was a very intelligent individual. My mom knew the mother of one of the other boys. In that month of January of that year, that small little town of Salina had more deaths than any other place in Oklahoma. Thank God Sissy was not involved with any of these people.

Sissy, for the first year in college, drove back and forth each day to Northeastern. Also, the subject material was getting harder; Sissy needed to stay there to get her work done. College was hard for Sissy. She did not make good grades in high school. I hardly saw Sissy when she stayed at Northeastern in college. When I left for OSU, I saw her less and less. We could not talk on the phone because it was too expensive. The first week I was at OSU, I became so lonesome I didn't know what to do. Mom called Roger to come and get me, which he did. Sissy had a car, so she could come back home anytime. As time went on, I was less lonesome. Bob and Loretta Piguet were at Stillwater also. I went to see them every Friday afternoon. Then I would head to the library until midnight and then possibly go to a dorm where we could study as long as we needed to. There were two guys that many times I would study with. Both of them were in engineering. From what I understand, the engineering school at OSU is excellent. One was named Steve, and the other one was Fitzgerald but we called him Fitz. Both were highly intelligent. Fitz had pimples all over his face, but he was a very likeable guy.

At this time, Sissy and I would see each other at Thanksgiving and Christmas and some in the summer the first and second year. After about three years at Northeastern, she was accepted at the University of Missouri in speech pathology. Sissy relocated because almost all of her time was dedicated to studying speech pathology and going to class.

While at the University of Missouri at Rolla, she met Robert Steadum. They dated off and on for about two years and eventually got married in Salina. My girlfriend, Linda, went to the wedding with me. That was Linda's first time in Oklahoma.

Sissy and I would try to come home at the same time. Getting a telephone was a big deal. Sissy and I would run around saying, "Ring, ring." Dad did not catch on to what was going on. Dad came home and found out that we had had a phone installed. This was important for Mom so she could keep up with what was happening with us. She would then tell Dad. I would call Mom at least one time per week and sometimes two to three times per week. I might have called Mom around one, one thirty, or two o'clock when I would get very lonesome. I usually got a letter from Mom every week. She would usually put $40 in the letter. Mom would keep me informed about what was going on in Salina. I would occasionally call Mom early in the morning, around 4:00 a.m. Many times I would have been studying all night long. I told Dad, "Sissy and I are going to be going to college. We need the ability to communicate with you. You need a way to communicate with us other than the nasty pay phone on Main Street. The pay phone is not an option for me to communicate with you and Mom. This is going to be an incredible way for Mom to communicate with Sissy and me. I am sure Mom will tell you about our conversations."

CHAPTER 6

Lige

Lige, my cousin, was three years old when I was born. We all lived in a farmhouse where Grandma, Lige, and Lillie Mae lived. We lived there for about eighteen months, after which we (Mom, me, and Sissy) all took a train to Ventura, California, where Dad was. When we went to Grandma's house, Lige and Lillie Mae were also there most of the time. When we moved back to Oklahoma, I was about three and a half years old. This was a good age to play with Sissy and Lige. We lived in Salina. Mom would call this man she called Wild Bill to take us to see Grandma, Lige, and Lillie Mae for the day. We then had a lot of good playing time. We loved to play in the barn. We knew this was forbidden territory. Frequently, Sissy and Lige would try to hide from me. I caught Lige standing in the kitchen door leading outside. He was not looking at me, and I ran as fast as I could and pushed him down the steps. He got up crying and went running to Lillie Mae, his mother. He told her that I pushed him out the back door "kackerds" meaning "backwards." I told Aunt Lilly that they were trying to run away from me and they would not let me play with them.

When Lige and Sissy started school, first grade for both, this markedly curtailed our visitation to Grandma's house. Mom and I would go to Grandma's house around one time a month. Lige, Lillie Mae, and Grandma would come to the house in Salina for a day, occasionally. From then on, we did not see much of Lige. Sissy went to Salina public school, and Lige went to Pryor public school.

When he was old enough to drive, he bought a very nice Chevrolet. He would drag Main and Salina and Pryor; it was one of the only things to do. At that time, Lige was a chain-smoker. He did not have a girlfriend. He went to school until the tenth grade and quit school. When he could, he enlisted in the Marines. There were papers that he needed to have filled out for entrance to the Marines. Interestingly enough, Jeff Dobbs completed them for Lige. Jeff Dobbs, Daddy and Anne's half brother, was a captain in the Marines and served in the Marines for around twelve and a half years. After Lige went to boot camp, he was sent to Vietnam; our contact with Lige was very minimal. Prior to him going to boot camp, Mom would occasionally hear from him either in person or by letter. Mom would usually pass the info to me and Sissy by phone. Nobody thought he would make it through boot camp, but he did.

Lige served two tours in Vietnam. Toward the end of the second tour, he was shot in the right leg. They were out on patrol in Vietnam when the group stopped to rest. There was a new marine in the group, and Lige was not getting along very well with this individual. The new marine leaned his rifle up against a small tree. The new marine was not following protocol. Somehow, the rifle fell from the tree, firing and hitting Lige in the right leg. The shot was so traumatic that the tibia was also fractured. He had to be airlifted by helicopter. He had an honorable discharge from the Marines on October 31, 1968. Lige suffered from post-traumatic stress disorder, depression, and anxiety after his discharge from the Marines.

Later in life, Lige did contact the person who shot him in the leg. Lige said that the other man said he did not remember shooting Lige in the leg. Lige asked him if he wanted to be in a film about Vietnam, and the man responded no. Lige told him to "have a good life," and he hung up.

Lige lived in Los Angeles for forty years starting in 1968. He worked in the LA area after he recovered from the gunshot wound. He worked for LA County as a custodian. He worked for nine and a half years in this job. He then started work with Lockheed as an expediter and worked there for seventeen and a half years. His job was highly secretive. Even today, talking about this, he is not able to give any details about his job. He moved to Montana and lived there from 2008 to 2012. He said the weather was so bad in Montana that he hardly made it outside the house for five to six months. The brush fires in California had been terrible. It was not a very good place to live. The same year Mom died, 2012, he came back to Locust Grove, Oklahoma, to live. His home in Montana was rented out by two nuns. We made contact when I was cleaning out Mom's house in Salina. I think we both had changed a lot over those years.

Lige was married twice. He met both of his wives at work. He had two children with his first wife, whom he was with for four and a half years, Victoria Lilliana Morten, thirty-seven, and Phillip William Morten, thirty-nine. He now has two grandchildren, Tory Adams, five, and Benjamin William Adams, two. Lige said that the second marriage was approximately four and a half years long. He came home one day and told his second wife that he did not love her anymore and that he was leaving ASAP (as soon as possible).

One time when Lige was visiting Oklahoma, he thought he could detect some dementia in his mom. He was concerned that she was living alone. He took his mother back to California with him. She lived with him for five years and died in 1998 when she was eighty-eight (she was born in 1910). We think she hardly ever got outside, though Lillie Mae went walking in the house for exercise one to two times per day. She never talked to anybody from Oklahoma, and my mom never saw Lillie Mae again. The dementia got worse to the point that she also had severe coronary artery disease and chronic obstructive pulmonary disease (COPD). She died with severe COPD. Lige had his mother cremated. I am sure cremation was a lot cheaper than having her body shipped back by train; however, Lillie Mae wanted to be buried next to her husband, Walter Morton, in Pryor Cemetery. My mother was in total disagreement with this. She did not want to see her sister cremated. Lige did bring the ashes back to Oklahoma. He hired a preacher and had the ashes scattered around the site of the old farmhouse and the cellar.

Walter, Lillie Mae's husband and Lige's dad, was born in 1896. He was in the army and served in World War I and II. I do not remember him at all, although there is a story told that I occasionally would go to the chicken house and get two eggs that I would crack, and then I would say, "Now." I would crack six to eight eggs before Walter would stop me. I was lucky that I did not run into a snake because the chicken house is a favorite place for snakes. They love the eggs.

Lige was also into acting; he was recently in a play called *The Wake of Light*. He went to Georgia to receive an award at the end of 2019. Lige was in a public service film too. In the ad, everybody was concerned with what the children were watching. During that time, there were controls on the TV where one could block what a child could watch. Lige would come into the room, dressed in black with a chain saw, ready to show the children an R-rated movie. Then the mother would tell him that he was blocked. Lige would display extreme disappointment. The film ran for around five years. The lady was "the Boss," and Lige, in black, played "the Slasher."

Lige is still living in Locust Grove, Oklahoma, at the present time, 2020. He is doing exceptionally well. We stay in contact quite frequently. He recently sold his house in Montana.

CHAPTER 7
Ann and Ed Hornbeck

Ann was Dad's full-blooded sister. Ann married at a young age. She suffered a lot of beatings and mental anguish. That marriage lasted about two years. She developed breast cancer, which was treated with a mastectomy. She never had a relapse. Ann worked at the fire station in Tulsa, where she lived. She met Ed Hornbeck, who was a firefighter. After they got married, he did not work anymore. I really do not know why he did not work. He had lived with his father in a house in Tulsa. I think his father suffered from depression. Ed Hornbeck always had a very nice car and was able to go on vacation. They drove to California to visit people out there two to three times per year. Dad and Ann had five half sisters and one half brother. They were all living in California. Almost all of the half sisters would drive back to Oklahoma to visit at least once a year. Dad's half brother, Jeff, came back to Oklahoma two to three times per year also. He was a captain in the Marines.

Ann and Ed came to our house every Christmas Eve and many times Christmas, the next day. They brought two to three gifts per person every Christmas. Mom made turkey if we could afford it. If not, we had fried chicken, which was excellent. I went hunting by myself. I was probably about ten years old at that time. Can you imagine the gun laws now that would have prevented me from doing this? It was probably two Christmases that we did not have enough money for a turkey. I went hunting by myself for turkeys, geese, but did not see any. Ann and Ed would come back on Christmas, December 25, to see all the toys that we got. One was a BB gun. Ed asked me if I wanted to shoot it. I said, "Yes." There was a fifty-five-gallon metal can that was frequently used by people in that area to burn trash. Ed told me to get my BB gun, and we would go out shooting. This, I did. There was a fifty-five-gallon metal can that was not too far from us. The BB gun shot very well and was very accurate. Ed and I did not see anybody outside that Christmas when we were shooting the BB gun that Mom and Dad had got for me.

One Christmas, there was a lot of snow, which kept Ann and Ed at home rather than coming to our house. Sissy and I were so disappointed. We did not have a phone for them to call and let us know that they had gotten a lot of snow. We did the usual, lots of presents on December 24, which we played with the next day. Ann and Ed came over the next day without a problem.

Ann and Ed also liked to occasionally come over on a Saturday and go walking in the woods looking for sassafras. Dad bought twenty-five chicken fryers. Ann and Ed wanted to buy all twenty-five. Dad thought we should keep at least five fryers for us. Mom, Sissy, and I killed and dressed all twenty chickens. We did keep five fryers for us. Sissy and I helped a lot. Our job was to pull all the feathers off after they were dipped in extremely hot water. Mom did this on a Sunday. They sold them for $2 a chicken, boy did that help us financially.

I remember that we had a party over at Auntie Ann's house on a Saturday. I remember Gloria and Roy coming over with their three children, Richard, Judy, and Gary; we did not play with them. I remember it being very difficult for Gary to be nice. He was throwing some rocks at a car, and he was chastised for doing this. All in all, things went fairly well.

In the spring of 1958, when I was ten years old, Ann and Ed were in an automobile accident traveling to California. Ed was driving; he was killed and Ann suffered a severe concussion. For some reason, Ann did not display a lot of grief or depression regarding the death of Ed. We thought this was unusual. Our whole family attended the funeral for Ed. Ann would occasionally come over to Salina to see me, Dad, Sissy, and Mom. Ann would occasionally come over, but not like before. We still walked in the woods. Sometimes, one to two times a month. For some reason, there was not much interaction between Ann and me and Sissy. Ann did not go to California very often either. After Ed's death, she was able to buy her own home. I think that Ed's dad took his son's death very hard. I was not the only one who agreed; it was all in the family that we were having problems with Ed's death. Ann and Ed did not have any children.

Ann went back to work. She again married a firefighter. He was older. They did a lot of traveling, and they would frequently go to California. They hardly came to our house for some reason. Therefore, we hardly saw Ann and her husband; I don't remember his name. Ann was a beautiful lady, plus she had a wonderful personality. Furthermore, she aged very well. She did not develop any signs of dementia. I don't know about Ann's intake of alcohol. I can certainly say I never saw Daddy drink a beer or any form of alcohol whatsoever. Oscar, his dad, was apparently an alcoholic. Everybody that met my sister thought she and Ann were daughter and mother. Oscar Yarborough must have had some good genes, other than the alcoholism.

Auntie Ann, as we called her, could have had a much younger man than whom she married. Her husband died after two years of marriage. She was alone again. The only kinfolk she had in Tulsa was a half sister named Sylvia. She occasionally saw Mom. She was diagnosed with cancer; where, I don't know. She was taken care of by Sylvia. She gave to Sylvia her power of attorney as well as her finances. When Auntie Ann died at age eighty-four, Sylvia transferred all of Auntie Ann's money to her account. This was approximately $250,000. There were all the California people that came back for the funeral. I did not because I was at school.

There were all the California people that came back for the funeral and to get as much as they possibly could from Auntie Ann's estate. The half sisters were absolutely apoplectic over what happened, the way everyone was loading up her belongings and stealing them. Mom and

Sissy told me that Sylvia was not at the funeral. Mom and Sissy went; Dad and I did not go. Apparently, Auntie Ann had bought herself a new Cadillac. I guess this was taken by Eddie Gene. The rest was gotten by everybody else. Ann's house was empty by nighttime. Sissy and I received about $1,500, not nearly what we should have. Sissy and I were full-blooded relatives.

Sylvia enjoyed finding the family tree. She did a good job at this. Her husband, Bud, developed Alzheimer's and was not helpful whatsoever. For some reason, she died suddenly of questionable causes, a sudden death with no explanation.

There was a basketball camp at Oral Roberts University in Tulsa. Ann and Ed said they would enjoy having me to stay with them. Ed could drive me back and forth. It was very well attended. This happened during the summer after tenth grade in high school. There were several coaches there to observe the teams that were playing. I noted one morning that Oral Roberts himself was there looking at the talent. Oral Roberts came up to me and wanted me to come to ORU and play basketball. He was, as he said, developing a sports program for both males and females. He was in the process of doing this with baseball too. He said both teams would be Division I. He wanted me to come to his office the next day. He was a very charismatic man. He told me all about ORU. I told him that I had already been accepted to OSU and that I was in the premed program. I also told him that I thought I would get a better chance of getting into medical school if I graduated from OSU instead of ORU. I told him that I would like to think about this for a few days and that I would call him. After three days, I met with him again and told him that I had decided to go to OSU. I told him that I decided to go to OSU. I could tell that he was very disappointed. He told me that if I changed my mind, all I would have to do is call him. The other important aspect of our conversation is that he said I would obtain my degree without any money, meaning a scholarship. He also said I could go to ORU for free.

Sissy and I loved to have Auntie Ann and Ed over. There was a lot of interaction with us. They talked and played with us but did not treat us like adults. I think Sissy and I held them in high esteem. I will never forget the day that Sissy and I were baptized. We were both baptized on the same day. We were baptized by Mr. Baldrigee. Little did we know that Uncle Ed and his father were at our house to take us to Spavinaw fishing. Mom said we could go. We fished from a boat dock. We probably caught thirty-plus perch. All were kept. Mom knew exactly how to handle the fish after watching Ed clean them. I was able to clean the fish too. We had an incredible meal. We had everything from the garden—lettuce, carrots, onions—in a salad. Mr. Hornbeck had a great time. Ed did a lot of filming. There is a thirty-second film of Sissy and me running. Sissy and I had to have either Mom or Dad make sure there were no bones in the fish. They would quite frequently have to chew up the fish and then give it to me or Sissy. The reason for this was a kid in Salina had a fish bone in his throat, and he died because of it. That's why they were so careful with us eating the fish.

I find it difficult to think that Ann would live in a tent on the banks of Grand River. Jeff's wife, Ruby, also my grandmother, was living in Salina in a house. Dad and Jeff would fish and sell the fish. How long Dad did this was questionable. I would like to know how Auntie Ann and Dad, GW, played together and associated with each other. Auntie Ann did graduate from Salina High School. Dad did not. I also find it interesting that Jeff, my stepgrandfather, and Ruby, my maternal grandmother, had six children. Maybe this was brought about by not having access to birth control.

How cool would it have been if Auntie Ann and Ed would have taken me and Sissy to Tulsa to spend the night and possibly go to a movie. Someone put in a movie theater in Salina. The first movie was Ma and Pa Kettle, which Sissy, Mom, and I went to. I don't think there was a voice reel to this movie. It was certainly in black and white. Dad declined going to the movie. I think it cost $0.10 to get in. We also got popcorn and Coke as a treat. The theater lasted about two years and then closed. Later on, a teacher from the high school opened it again. He really did bring some very good movies to town. He brought several Elvis movies to be shown; these were a big hit. After about a year, he also had to close the theater when I was ten in 1959. The last night he had a drawing for $25. Sissy won the money. I met her at the back of the movie, and we ran home as fast as we could. We both could not believe it! The only other place to watch a movie was in Pryor. Our Sunday school class, which was made up of all boys, had a party about every two months; almost always we went to Pryor for a movie. The very first one was the *Ten Commandments*. I probably saw that movie four times. Still, it is my favorite movie of all time. Almost all of the churches in that part of Oklahoma went to the movie theater in Pryor. To this day, it is the most favored movie, and the movie theater is still open in 2019.

CHAPTER 8

Syncope

I was seven years old in second grade, and one morning, as I tried to stand to get ready for school, I could not stand. As I attempted to stand, I would lose consciousness and fall to the floor. I told Mom that I was extremely weak. She took one look at me and knew that we had to go to the hospital. She knew there was something wrong. She immediately went to the pay phone on Main Street and called Jeff, who usually took us to Grandma's house to visit. I had to crawl to the car. I had a very difficult time doing this. I could not sit up. I had to lie across the back seat. The car ride was somewhat painful. I was taken to Grand Valley Hospital in Pryor. They told Mom that I was severely anemic and that I probably had leukemia. They stated that they could not help me. They suggested that I go to Hillcrest Hospital in Tulsa. In the emergency room, it was found out that I had a profound anemia, and I needed to be admitted for evaluation. Shortly after I was admitted, I received some blood that made me feel much better. I was able to walk again without syncope. Multiple studies were done on me. Nothing was found in the GI tract. Back then, there was nothing like the endoscopic studies done now. Mom and Dad were told that there must be something in the GI tract bleeding every now and then. One day, the nurse came in and told me that I needed to go for another test. I was taken to a very cold room and told to get on the table. My hands and feet were tied. A drill was placed on my sternum, and they began to drill. The pain was very intense. They then placed a large syringe over the hole and began to suction. This also was very painful. Eventually, they were done. I was taken back to my room. I cried myself to sleep.

My chest hurt with every breath that I took. This was a very difficult procedure to do. When drilling through the sternum, the drill comes very close to the heart and lungs. If the drill comes into contact with the heart or lungs, the patient may die. While I was in the hospital for a week, no one visited me. Mom did not stay in the hospital with me but went back and forth. Mom and Dad were told I did not have leukemia. Upon discharge, a definite diagnosis was not found. They felt that there could be a polyp in the intestines that would occasionally bleed. I was not to play any contact sports, and I needed to be on a soft diet. I was able to shoot hoops in the backyard. I missed about two weeks of school; I was so far behind. A major assignment was to learn the capitals of all the states. I didn't think I would learn them.

About a year later, I began to have gastric pain. The pain was terrible but was partially relieved by eating and ingesting baking soda. Mom eventually took me to see Dr. Cameron in Pryor; he was our family physician. He did an upper GI and found a duodenal ulcer. I was given medication, which stopped the pain. I asked Dr. Cameron if I could play football, and he said yes, but to let the ulcer heal first. I couldn't have heard better news. Now, I could get back to playing my three sports.

Chapter 9
Monroe, My Friend

Monroe was a man about 5'10" and very strong. He had no fat on himself at all. It was all muscle. He had two mules, Mike and Sam. He went around town plowing people's gardens and fields. One of those gardens was our garden. I knew of no one around town that had any other means of plowing their gardens; they all depended on Monroe. One morning, as he was plowing our garden, I went out to observe. It was a very hot day. I was nine years old. Monroe was a chain-smoker of Camels and Red Man chewing tobacco. Sometimes he would have saliva, discolored by the chewing tobacco, running down his chin. He called me over and asked if I wanted to try plowing. I did. The key was to keep the sharp part of the plow deep into the ground. I could do this by pushing forward and by standing on the plow. Monroe would walk behind me if I got into trouble. Another hard part was turning the plow at the end of the row. Mike and Sam knew just what to do. Monroe would holler, "Turn, turn, turn!" as he would whistle loudly. When we were finished, I gave Mike and Sam some cold water to drink. I also poured cold water on their neck and back. They seemed to love this.

Monroe asked if I wanted to "go" tomorrow. Mom said, "Don't get in the way, and you know you have to get your chores done."

I replied, "I know." I got up at daybreak, had breakfast, and got my chores done. I was sore all over because plowing was a very hot and hard job. We started around seven o'clock in the morning and worked until around six o'clock in the evening. There were certain gestures that Mike and Sam knew, and I had to learn them too. I had to make sure that both were pulling the same. A slap on the butt with the reins would correct if one was doing most of the work. If the owner of the garden that we were plowing needed their small barn cleaned out, I could put the manure in the wagon; therefore, I did not have to go and get the manure with the wheelbarrow. I cannot believe that I cleaned out all of those barns without a face mask. Day after day, Monroe and I plowed people's gardens and fields. My clothes would be wet with sweat. We did not have an indoor bathroom to take a shower or a bath. Instead, I would clean up with a washcloth and a pail of water. If Dad wanted to play catch in the afternoon, and he did like to do this quite frequently, I would go out and catch. Even though I was very tired, I enjoyed this also. Occasionally, I would go out and shoot hoops by myself. Sissy was usually playing with some of her friends. By nine o'clock in the evening, King and I were asleep on the floor. I grew to love Mike and Sam. Every day at the end of the day, I would give them oats and cold water. I would pour cold water on their necks and backs and brush them down. They loved this. At the end of the day, I could sense that they knew that this was part of the routine. Monroe would give me a dollar a day for my work. After about eight weeks, all of the gardens and fields were plowed. For the latter part of eight weeks of plowing of the fields and gardens, he would give me two dollars instead of one dollar. By around eight weeks, all of the gardens and fields were plowed that people had requested. After this was finished, I still, day after day, went to visit Sam and Mike. I would give them oats, followed by a cold bath and brushing.

I had not seen Monroe for quite some time. One day, as I was feeding Mike and Sam, I could see Monroe walking toward the barn. I could tell something was wrong. He looked disheveled and emaciated. He said that he was not feeling good and that he was going to the hospital. He asked if I could take care of Mike and Sam. I replied that I would. Monroe lived in a small cabin that had only two rooms. He had a potbellied stove to heat the cabin in the wintertime. We had the very same thing at our house, a potbellied stove. He had an outhouse and a good well. Day after day, I would visit Mike and Sam twice a day. After about ten days, as I was feeding Sam and Mike, there was a car that pulled up, and an individual got out and went into the log cabin. I immediately went to see what was going on. I asked the man why he was in Monroe's house. He replied that Monroe had died and that he needed to get some important papers. I walked, slowly, back to the barn in disbelief. I knew something was wrong the day Monroe told me he was not feeling well. I sat down on a stool in the barn and began to cry. I don't know the cause of Monroe's death, but with his tobacco use, it was probably a heart attack or lung cancer. He was about fifty-five years old. I was six years old.

My first encounter with death came at six years of age; I did not know much about death. My first encounter with death was when a white cat named Puff died. I kept him in the cellar house. Every day after school, I would let him out to play. One day, I opened the door, and Puff was lying on the floor. I hollered, "Puff!" but he did not respond. I ran back to the kitchen where Mom was. I hollered to Mom that there was something wrong with Puff. We ran back to the cellar house.

Mom touched Puff, but there was no response. Mom turned to me and said, "Sonny, come here," as she hugged me tightly. She said, "Sonny, Puff is dead." She told me that Puff was in heaven. Mom and Dad buried Puff behind the cellar house, where most of the dogs and cats were buried. There was a sense of sadness every day as I went out the back door to play basketball. I missed opening that cellar door and seeing Puff run around outside. But as Mom told me, he was in heaven, and that helped me to feel less sad.

As I sat on the stool in the barn, crying, I just could not imagine never seeing Monroe again. We had spent the last eight weeks together, almost daily. We worked very hard plowing the land. Monroe and I talked about many things while riding on the wagon. I learned a lot from Monroe. He had worked very hard throughout his life. He had told me that he had no family that cared about him. He had a sister who lived in Texas that he had not seen in many years. I could see Monroe tearing up while talking about this. He stated that his mother and father were deceased. I doubt if Monroe even had a funeral. As I sat there on the stool, it struck me, what was going to happen to Mike and Sam? I walked home slowly. There were a lot of things going on in my head.

At supper that night, I told Mom and Dad that Monroe had died. I asked them if I could keep Mike and Sam. I told them that I knew how to take care of them. They told me that there was no way we could keep Mike and Sam. I started crying, and I begged them to let me keep them. I just did not want Mike and Sam to go away. I got up from the supper table and went to the hay house where my dogs were. I spent that night in the hay house. I cried myself to sleep. The next day, I went to visit Mike and Sam. I walked very slowly to Monroe's house. My worst fears were true. Mike and Sam were gone. I began crying profusely as I walked to the barn. I sat on the stool for a long time. I could sense their presence. There was someone in the log cabin. I walked over and asked the man if he knew what happened to Mike and Sam. He said they were picked up and sold. I asked him if he knew if they were sold together or separately. He stated that he thought they were sold together. He said they were two good mules. I replied, "Yes, they were." I could not believe that I would never see Sam and Mike again.

I walked home slowly. I needed to know more about heaven. When I got home, I asked Mom to tell me more about heaven and what it was. She replied that heaven was a place where good boys and girls went. I asked her if Monroe went to heaven. She replied yes. For a long time after this, I would ask Mom if I was a good boy and if I was going to go to heaven. She would always reply, "Yes."

CHAPTER 10
The Town of Salina, Oklahoma

In 1949, the town of Salina, Oklahoma, was an impoverished small town of about nine hundred people in Northeastern Oklahoma. Mom and Dad moved to Salina two different times. The first time Mom and Dad moved was after they got married. Dad could not find any gainful employment. His mother and half sisters wanted him to come to California to work on an orchard. The pay was good and steady. Dad would send money back to Mom. Mom had to move back to the farm because they could not pay for the rent. Three months later, Mom delivered me. Mom decided to go to California. We lived in a small house on the orchard. From the beginning, Mom and Dad wanted to move back to Oklahoma. After about two years, they decided to make the move back to Salina. This time, they stayed until their deaths. At that time, Salina really did not have much to offer.

Dad did buy the house for $1,200. Mom really liked the location because it was central to many things, like employment, church, laundry, and so on. They did not have any transportation. Mom and Dad did not drive. The house sat on four big lots. The house had electricity and running cold water. The house was heated by either wood or coal (whichever was cheaper) with a big potbellied stove. The toilet was outside and attached to a chicken house. Having a big garden, as well as chicken to eat, somewhat blunted the horrible times of poverty.

On Main Street, and one block away from our house, there were four grocery stores. Mr. McClay, one of the grocery store owners, hired

Mom to work for two days out of the week. This soon went up to five days a week. Mom got paid $3 a day as well as a discount for food.

Mom met a lady at church who owned a laundromat. She would be happy to get a ride to the laundry. I remember Mom lifting me up and putting me on a laundry machine. She gave me some cars and trucks to play with. I remember seeing the hoses that went right into the river. What an environmental mess! The First Baptist Church was across the street from our house. The bus to Pryor stopped in the middle of Main Street. Other than food, the four grocery stores in Salina did not sell much of anything else. We did have a secondhand store, which helped with some of the necessities throughout the year. Pryor, ten miles away, had stores with more items for sale. If we went to Pryor, it was only one or two times a year. One of those times was about a week before school started. This was mainly for school shoes and clothes. I would usually wear out the shoes, and then we had to go to the secondhand store. I always wore Wrangler jeans. This was because the stores in Pryor did not carry Levi's. The jeans in Salina were secondhand. I was the only boy that wore Wrangler in the entire school. I also had Haggar pants; Haggar pants are men's dress pants. We had to get one coat a year. The coats in the secondhand store were not very good.

When we needed to go to Pryor for items we could not get in Salina, we would take the bus. We had to buy the ticket for the bus at the drugstore. The bus went to Pryor from Salina at eight and back again at four thirty. There was a very dangerous bridge that the bus went across over the Grand River. The river was unpredictable. There would be a lot of water or possibly none at all. When there wasn't any water, there were always sixty-five to eighty-pound catfish (these were what Jeff liked because he could gig them with a fork. He would go to Main Street, where he would sell the fish he had just caught.) The dangerous bridge only accepted one-way traffic. The bottom of the bridge consisted of loose wooden planks. When Mom wanted to go to Grandma's house she would call this man whom she called Wild Bill. He would pick us up in the afternoon. It was not so bad going over the bridge in a car;

going by bus was scary because of the noises the bridge would make. One scene that is in my mind is of one of my buddies boarding the bus when he was on his way to Vietnam. He had a big duffel bag filled with items needed for Vietnam. We had played baseball together. He made it through two tours without many problems. Mentally, that was a different story. I think that the bus went to Claremore and to Fort Smith, Arkansas.

Not many people liked Ruby, Dad's mother. Every time Sissy or I saw her, she required a kiss on the lips. She always chewed snuff, which would get on my lips and in my mouth. Why she married Jeff Dobbs and had six more children is beyond all. They probably didn't have access to any birth control.

CHAPTER 11

The House in Salina

When Mom and Dad came back from California to Oklahoma, they went to Salina, where Dad got a job with Mr. Childress doing carpenter work around town. They also rented a house in Salina from Mr. Childress for $4 a month. It was a clapboard house with four rooms. It was heated by wood or coal in a potbellied stove, which stuck out into the living room. There was no heat in the kitchen except for burning kerosene, which did not produce much heat. In the winter, there was only one room in our house that was heated, and that room was poorly heated. If Sissy and I wanted to play a game, we had to put on our coats. Even with our coats on, the cold air was coming in from the windows and so on. We, for a short period of time, had electric blankets to warm up with. My bed was in the living room near the potbellied stove. I had to make sure that the coals were still present come morning. There were two chairs on each side of the stove—this was about the only place that was warm. When we washed up, this is where it was done. We did not have an indoor toilet. About 9:00 p.m., we all went outside to relieve ourselves.

A house was built over the cellar. The cellar was fairly good. It was not as good a cellar as Grandma had because we took very good care of the cellar at Grandma's such that it had no pests; we had pests in our cellar at the house in Salina. The cellar was right outside to the back of the kitchen, about twenty feet away from the back door. We had to go outside to enter it. The cellar, in the summertime and springtime, was used a lot. Because Dad had been struck by lightning in the past, he was in the cellar along with us when there was thunder and lightning. Sometimes we were there all night long and into the morning hours, into our school day.

The house was on a big lot across from the First Baptist Church and one block from Main Street, where there were four different grocery stores. The large lot allowed for Dad to build a chicken house, the selling of eggs, and a nice big garden. There was a big chicken house already present on the property with an outhouse toilet attached. Turning over toilets was a favorite thing at Halloween. They could not do that with our toilet. I am sure that they tried. Mom was afraid that Mr. Childress was going to sell the house. Years later, Dad bought the house for $1,200. Anytime I think about the house in Salina, the song "The House That Built Me" by Miranda Lambert comes to mind. Mom told me I could barely climb up the two front steps when we moved in.

We started a garden. We had to dig up the Bermuda grass, which was really hard to do. Dad wanted to fertilize the garden with manure. There were several people around town who had a horse or cow, and they would notify. Dad said I was to go and get the poop out of the barn. Talk about a hard job; it was hot! The manure was sometimes very hard, requiring a pick and shovel to get it out. Frequently, there was a lot of dust, and I wonder what I breathed in by doing all of this stuff. I was so embarrassed when someone in my grade saw me go down the road with a wheelbarrow full of poop. I would therefore get up shortly after daybreak and work for two to three hours. I figured that it would be unlikely for one of my classmates to see me during that period of time.

Dad also had three compost piles; usually, they also had to be turned over, and the stench was horrible. One time, the stench was noted a block away on Main Street. When we went to the cellar, I would grab the salt shaker and pour salt on the leeches, which were everywhere in the cellar. Many times, we went to school from the cellar. We had no radar to help guide us as to bad weather coming or going.

Mom, as mentioned before, had a kerosene stove. It was my job to get the kerosene. There was a five-gallon container that I had to make sure it was at least one-half full.

There was also a pitching rubber and home plate in front of our house. As a kid, I had been hit in the head and chest and other parts of my body with Dad's knuckleball. He had an unbelievable amount of movement. He had a good knuckleball and good curveball. There would be kids and adults that would stop and watch us play catch. This was probably why Sam Baker put me as catcher. I could quite easily see that there was no changing of the stripes. I still think I would have been a good pitcher also. Dad also put up a ten-foot basketball goal, one that the guys who ruined my other ones would not be able to jump nearly high enough to get to. Dad also put up a basketball goal at the regulation height of eight feet. One Saturday, there was a group of older kids that came by and tried to dunk the ball. In the process of trying this, they tore my basketball goal up. As Dad came out, they drove off. It was not long before a stronger goal was put up in the same place. This one was ten feet, regulation height too. We put the goal post deep into the ground. This I liked. I could shoot hoops by myself. I could also play imaginary one-on-one or teams.

There would occasionally be a kid that would come by, look at how high it was, and then walk on. Some kids, I wouldn't even give them the basketball. We put the goal post deep into the ground. This I liked.

I want to thank my father for leading me in the direction of sports. Like I mentioned, we would play catch in the afternoons after supper; we obviously played football, which everybody really liked. There had to be a bit of athleticism that Dad saw in me; that was made stronger and stronger every time that we played catch. I thank my father for that.

Before too long, Mom went to the church and told Mr. Baldrigee she wanted to teach a Sunday school class. She was given a class of five- to six-year-olds, and she taught for sixty-five years. She taught generations of kids; mothers and husbands wanted their kids to be taught by Ida Bell in a Sunday school class.

Mom really liked Mr. Baldrigee. Mr. and Mrs. Baldrigee had four children, the youngest being Bobby, who was one year older than me. The Baldrigees lived in the parsonage immediately in the back of our church. Sissy and I were baptized by Mr. Baldrigee. Sissy and I were around twelve years of age. That was something that Mom really wanted to get done. I was relieved after I was baptized.

Mom did not like for Sissy and me to cross the road without her either taking us across or watching us as we crossed the road. We would immediately begin playing when we got to where the sidewalks were. It was incredible to have sidewalks that one could ride a bike on.

Mom made sure that Sissy and I went to church every time the church doors opened. During the hot days, there was a big fan at the front of the church. Water was used to help cool with the big fan. Handheld fans with pictures of Jesus helped to cool us further. When we went home, we had only the handheld fans to try and keep cool.

Mom was deeply religious. Mr. and Mrs. McClay were also members of the First Baptist Church. They lived close to the parsonage. There was another building, probably twenty-five to thirty yards from the main church, which gave us an excellent place to play football, baseball, and so on. If basketball was to be played, we would do it in our backyard. Mom was working at Mr. McClay's grocery store.

Mom loved this house. The house had electricity. The farm still did not have any electricity; lights were from coal oil lantern. They could not afford a TV. Instead, they bought a radio, which was our contact with the outside world. The outside world was not that important to me. I wanted to have a playmate other than Sissy. At this time, I still have the radio that was bought for the house.

CHAPTER 12
Sam Baker Baseball

Sam Baker was a slightly muscular short Cherokee Indian. There was no fat on Sam whatsoever. He was an electrician by trade. Sam was a type A personality when it came to baseball. Sam had a habit of making sure his pants were up by feeling with his forearm and rubbing his arm along the side of his body where his pants sat. He was a chain-smoker of Camel cigarettes with occasional Red Man chewing tobacco. Sam had two boys, Walter and James. They would come to our house, which was right across from the church. We would play baseball for about an hour before church. This was really fun and helpful in developing me as a "hard thrower." People would stop and watch us play. Walter, the younger boy, was a very good athlete. He was left-handed and ran very fast. He was two years older than me. I was eight years old at this time. His brother, James, was a good athlete but not as good as Walter. They were always very impressed as to how fast I could throw the ball.

One night after church, Sam asked Mother if I could play baseball over the summer with his team. He told her he was going to make two teams. Mom said it was okay. Sam knew that we did not have a car. He said he would come by and get me every day. Sam was able to get eleven kids on each team. The older team was made up of boys approximately two years older than those of us on the younger team. We started practice three days later. Mom had discussed this with Dad; he was okay with the idea.

I will never forget the first day of real baseball. I was anxious but ready to play. I came outside to wait for Sam to pick me up. Mother was working in the garden. I had a glove that we had bought at the secondhand store. I did not have a new bat; I had a bat that had seen better days. It had been broken and taped. I was staring at the ground as I could see out the corner of my eye Mom coming toward me. She grabbed me by the chin, turning my head toward her, and said "Sonny, look at me. You can play anywhere except catcher. Do you hear me?" I said, "Yes, Mom." And she gave me a hug.

Before long, Sam came and got me. We were heading toward the ballpark. I remember the anxiety increasing as we approached the ballpark. The only baseball I had ever played was "catch" as well as "sandlot" baseball with all rubber balls. I knew I had a very strong arm, but what about the rest of baseball? Would I be good enough to play the other parts of baseball? Sam talked to the entire team before we got started. He had rules that were established before we got started. If one did not follow them, then the person would be disciplined. Sam looked out of one eye. I do not know if he was blind in the other eye. He was left-handed and always had a Camel cigarette in the other hand. Frequently, Sam would be chewing Red Man tobacco. Sam told each kid where to play. Sam told me to play catcher. The anxiety that I felt was crippling. I could imagine nothing but Mom looking me in the eyes and telling me I could not play catcher. What was I to do? Tell Sam I could not play catcher? Sam told me there was a bag with some equipment in it. I walked slowly to the bag. My only hope was that maybe I was not good enough to play catcher. As I was emptying the bag, I could see a glove at the bottom of the bag; as I grabbed the glove, I could see the funny shape of it. I had never seen a glove like this before. The only equipment were a mask and chest protector, which had seen better days. Sam yelled to his older son that he should warm me up. I put on the equipment with the help of his son. I was ready to go. I had played catch with him before but not with this funny glove. It was round with a lot more padding compared with the other gloves.

He gave me some tips on playing catcher. He told me that if the ball hit the dirt before I could catch it, I should let it hit the chest protector. Why I was not picked to be a pitcher, I will never know. I regret that I never asked Sam that question. I probably missed half of the balls thrown to me. When I got behind the plate, soon there was a ball that hit home plate before I could catch it. I turned my head, and the ball hit me in the throat. God, that hurt! I did not think I could breathe. Sam asked me if I was okay. I replied yes. For probably a week, I could hardly swallow. From that time on, I let the ball hit me in the chest protector; this was not painful at all. We did not have metal bats; they were all wood. Furthermore, there were only four or five bats in total. If someone broke a bat, we put it back together with duct tape. All of the equipment was bought personally by Sam. At the end of practice, Sam asked me how I liked playing catcher. I replied, "Very much." I think he was pleased as to how well I played catcher. Sam took me home after practice. The view at our house from the road was such that one could see straight through the house. As I got out of the car, I could see Mom in the kitchen looking at me with her left hand on her hip, as if she wanted to know where I had played right away. I thanked Sam for the ride and said I would see him tomorrow. Instead of going to the house, I went to the hay house to see my dogs. I began to cry. I had not obeyed my Mother. I stayed in the hay house for a couple of hours. The dogs would always get as close to me as possible.

Eventually, I heard someone come out of the back door. It was Mom. She said, "Sonny, come to supper." I wiped away my tears and went to the kitchen. I ate everything in sight. Nothing was said until the end of supper. Mom asked, "How was baseball?"

I said, "Very good."

She asked, "Did you play catcher?" I began to cry. It was hard to say yes. Dad asked if I liked it, playing catcher. And I replied yes. I got up from the kitchen table and grabbed my basketball and went to the backyard to shoot baskets. About an hour later, Mom came to where I was shooting baskets. She said, "Sonny, come here." She gave me a big hug and told me that it was okay if I wanted to play catcher. She told me to be the best I can. I told her that I would. She then said, "I love you." I felt a ton of weight being lifted off of my shoulders. Within a week, there was a box that came from Sears. In it were a catcher's mitt, chest protector, shin guards, and face mask. I could not believe it. I know this was a drain on our money. To this day, I still have all of the above equipment.

Sam put me behind the plate, and I never played any other position. Day after day, I could tell I was getting better and better, not only playing catcher but also hitting. I loved playing catcher. I received very little training as a catcher. My training came mainly from hard knocks. I had developed into an excellent catcher very fast. Sam asked me if I could be the catcher for the older boys. Immediately I said yes. What would Mom and Dad say about this? Furthermore, my hitting was good, and there were very few people that could steal second base. But would the older boys accept me? I would hang around with Walter; he would protect me if needed. One boy did not. His name was Bobby Alberty. This was because I was a much better baseball player than him. He bullied me as much as he could. I would try to sit with Walter on bus trips. Bobby would not mess with Walter; he was obviously a coward. It got so bad that I started carrying a knife. He became so disruptive to the team that halfway through the season, he was let go. We did not miss him at all. I was standing next to Sam when Sam told him he was not on the team anymore. As I walked away, I started laughing.

At supper one night, I told Mom and Dad that Sam wanted me to be catcher for the older boys. I told Sam I would, and I thanked him. Mom and Dad stared at each other for the longest time. It was not in our family tradition to heap praise on one's accomplishments; however, I do think they were very proud. I got up and went to get the basketball and went to shoot baskets.

At that time in baseball, one could run into the catcher as hard as you could. After being hit hard a few times, I had to devise a plan to protect myself. I would hit them as hard as I could in front of the plate, and if

I could, I would slap them in the face with my glove as hard as I could. This sometimes resulted in fights. I always left my mask on, so therefore, I did not get hit in the face. The next time we played this team, they had better think twice about pulling this shit on me.

We had very good pitching on each team. Clarence Kingfisher for the younger team and Sam Bell for the older team. Both were Cherokee Native Americans. Sam was difficult to catch. He had a very good curveball as well as a fastball and changeup. His fastball had a lot of movement on it. Both were unbeaten for the two seasons.

We played forty-five to fifty very competitive games throughout those two seasons. That meant that I played twice that number. Sam would sit on his haunches and keep score. He would have one eye closed, a pen in his left hand and a Camel cigarette in his right hand. He always wanted me to sit beside him and tell him what was happening. Sam trusted me to call the games for both teams. Contrary to what my parents were afraid of, I did not get injured while playing catcher. Both teams were unbeaten for the two seasons. We played a lot of games in those two seasons. Why we did not play more than two seasons, I do not know. However, Clarence and I did play for three seasons; that is the subject of another chapter in this book: "Locust Grove Baseball." I learned a lot about baseball and life from Sam in those two seasons. He would frequently come and watch Clarence and me play when we were in high school. I did not see much of his sons after those two seasons of baseball. I really enjoyed playing catch with them, as well as playing catcher on the same team they played.

I will never forget the first game my mother and father attended. They sat in the front row. I hope that Dad knew that he had a big influence in regard to all of those afternoons playing catch when I was a little boy in the front yard. Also, it was the first game after Mom looked into my eyes and told me that I could play any position except catcher. Do you understand? A lot of things had changed since then. Most of these changes were positive changes. Dad never told me he loved me. He never told me I was a good baseball player. I do think they were very proud of me as to how I had developed into a very good baseball player. Dad just did not know how to express it. We won both games the day they came to see me play. After these two games, Mom and Dad came as often as they could to see me play.

Sam was an incredible man. I am so proud and honored that Sam asked my mother if I could play baseball for him.

The year preceding summer baseball is the summer I was plowing with Monroe. Not only this, but I had to dig up our garden and get the grass and roots out. These were two backbreaking jobs. This made me very strong. It did not matter how hot it was; these things had to be done. I would occasionally see this whitish substance on my jeans at the end of the day. It tasted like salt. It probably was salt from perspiration.

Who knows what would have happened if I had played summer baseball beyond these three summers. There were three junior colleges that wanted me to play baseball and basketball for them.

After playing summer baseball at Locust Grove, neither I nor Clarence played summer baseball again. Instead, I spent my summers cutting wood, hauling hay, and digging ditches. This made me very strong. Who knows what would have happened if I had played summer baseball.

At a basketball camp at Oral Roberts University between my sophomore and junior year, Oral Roberts pulled me aside and wanted me to come to his office the next day. This, I did. He told me that he had seen me play three different times and that he would like for me to come to ORU and play baseball and basketball.

Oral Roberts spoke with confidence and appeared very "strong" about his convictions, and he was believable and followed through on his promises. I told him I would think about this and get back in touch with him. I had my sights set on becoming a physician rather than playing baseball/basketball. Furthermore, I thought that if I made good grades at OSU, I would have a better chance to get into medical school compared with schooling at ORU. Also, I was going to be a walk on at

Oklahoma State in basketball anyway. I did meet with him again and told him the above. He said he was very disappointed and told me to please call him if I had a change of mind. I thanked him very much, and I told him I would. He told me I could go to ORU for free.

The baseball program in Salina has been excellent. There have been two boys drafted into the major leagues. Several boys received scholarships who otherwise would not have gone to college because of financial reasons. I know that Bob Baldridgee built a baseball program that Salina high school could be proud of. Hopefully, that tradition has continued. The baseball stadium in Salina is named Sam Baker State Baseball Stadium. There is not another individual that deserves his name on this baseball stadium. Sam got baseball started in Salina, and hopefully, it will continue; the stadium is still there.

At the end of the second baseball season, as I was sitting on the bench savoring all of the changes that had taken place over the last two years, I could see Sam walking toward me out of the corner of my eye. He said, "Sonny, stand up." as he handed me that "funny looking" glove. Sam said, "there is no catcher anywhere that deserves this more than you." Sam gave me a big hug. I was speechless. I was able to say, "Thank you, Sam." I sat back down and began to cry. I was able to tell Sam that I wanted to walk home and I would be okay. There was still a slight smell of leather to the glove. It was a long walk home; but I needed that. There were so many circumstances rolling through my mind. When I got home, I went to the hay house and laid with my dogs for a while. I always got some big licks from my dogs when I laid with them. At supper that afternoon I showed the funny glove to my Mom and Dad. I told them that Sam wanted me to have it. After supper, dad and I played catch with that funny glove one last time before retiring it.

Over the years I have worn out four different funny gloves. Every now and then I put one of them on and pound the pocket with my fist. I become mesmerized and so many circumstances start rolling through my brain. These catcher mitts are some of my most treasured items that I have from my childhood.

CHAPTER 13
Bobby Baldridgee

Mr. Baldridgee, who was the preacher at the First Baptist Church, which was one block away from our house, was a Cherokee Indian. Mr. Baldridgee and his wife had four children. The family lived in the parsonage. Bobby was one year older than me. The other three brothers and sisters were much older than Bobby and myself. The older siblings had no intention of playing with us. Because Sissy was also about one year older than me, we three played very nicely together. There was sidewalk around the church we could ride our bikes on. We played baseball, football, and basketball together. Sissy was much better at sports than most girls that came to play.

Bobby loved to go walking in the woods with the family, usually Mom, Dad, Sissy, and myself along with Bobby. I usually brought my BB gun, a .22-gauge rifle and a single-shot shotgun. If we saw a snake lying on the bluff, we usually shot it with the shotgun. Bobby and I would take turns shooting the snake. The shotgun had an incredible kick to it. Pooch and Spot, my dogs, usually went with us. We also usually brought a slingshot with us. This was also fun to use. We usually made ice cream before we went for a walk in the woods. The ice cream maker was packed with ice, and we would stir the ice cream until it was difficult to stir. We usually had supper; then we would have ice cream. It was so good. Bobby was invited because he helped stir the ice cream. He agreed that it was the best ice cream around. Pooch and Spot got a little bit of ice cream also.

There were plenty of rocks on the railroad tracks. We occasionally found Indian arrowheads. After walking quite a ways on the railroad track, we took a well-beaten path to the river. We had to walk cautiously on the trail; if we did not, we could fall headfirst. We had to be careful to make sure there were no snakes. Pooch loved to go swimming in the river. Bobby, Sissy, and I loved to play Cowboys and Indians. We all had arrows from the bodark tree. We had one rule that we had to abide by, which was we could not shoot at another individual's head. Not only would we play Cowboys and Indians with the bows and arrows, but also we would put up a target and see how we could well all use the bows and arrows.

We also had a teepee that we had outside the back door. We would occasionally spend the night in the teepee. Bobby loved doing this also. We all were afraid of the old man next door. We usually would start telling stories about him and other disturbing, crazy stories. We sometimes had to go inside and spend the night on the living room floor. The back door would be open and unlocked. If we got scared, we would go to the living room and sleep there, rather than in the tent. It helped to have Pooch and Spot in the tent with us. If we needed to do that.

When we got to the river, Dad most of the time would fish while we would eat our lunch. Bobby loved doing this also.

The church was a block from us. Mr. Baldridgee was the preacher. The parsonage was next to the church. Mom went to church there a few times. Mom really liked Mr. Baldridgee as a preacher and as a person.

Bobby and I played baseball and football in between the church and another building. If we started playing catch with either the baseball or football, there would be another four to six kids wanting to play. We would play whatever the majority of the kids wanted to play. We played basketball in our backyard. A lady by the name of Ms. McClay— lived close to the parsonage. She never had any children. She did not like having baseballs hit in her yard. We knew this, and we would intentionally try to hit the ball into her yard. This was counted as a home run. She occasionally would sit on her porch and get the balls if we hit them into her yard. Because of this, we had to have several balls. Almost every Saturday afternoon after the University of Oklahoma football game, we would have ten to fifteen kids that wanted to play flag football. Bobby was one of the individuals that we invited to play. Dad loved to play this game. The quarterback was usually me, Dad, or Bobby. We played the game until dark. Nobody ever got hurt. We had both boys and girls. We had a rule that every team had to have an equal number of girls.

We were very loud. People would come by to see what was happening. People on Main Street would stop and stare, watching what was happening. As darkness came, nobody wanted to stop. We had to eat, and the other important thing on Saturdays was the *Grand Ole Opry* at 9:00 p.m. As usual, in our house, all of the lights had to be off.

There was a major problem with the church. It began to lean to the left. There was no money to replace the church. There was a huge fan that used water to keep the congregation cool. We also had handheld fans with a picture of Jesus on them. These also helped. The congregation was asked to sit on the right side of the church because of the lean. Eventually, people in the church put large telephone poles on the left side of the church. In today's times, the church would have been condemned. If the church had fallen, it was likely that there would have been numerous casualties. This seemed to stabilize the church. I am uncertain if Mr. Baldridgee was the preacher at the church at that time or not. I do not think he was.

There was an incident where I was throwing spears high into the sky. They were coming down and landing into the ground. Sissy and Andrew Kay, her friend, were sitting on the porch. I threw a spear as high as I could, and it came down, landing on Andrew's left upper eyelid. We pulled the spear out; there was some very mild bleeding.

The eyeball itself was not involved, thank goodness. We probably would have been sued if the eye itself had been involved. Dad found out and told me to get all of my spears and put them on the burn pile; this was done ASAP.

When we were not playing at the church, we played in our backyard. There were four to six men from the telephone office that would come over to play basketball with us. They loved doing this, and we loved having them. Bobby frequently played. We always played until dark. I was really improving my basketball skills at that time. Sissy had a friend in the twelfth grade who would come over almost every day after school. She and Sissy played first team varsity basketball with Salina. She was Sharon Alberty, a very pretty girl. They would usually come to play basketball in the backyard. There were a couple of telephone office men's wives who told Mom that we were stealing their husbands. They were kidding. Mom acknowledged that their husbands loved to play basketball with us. Sharon Alberty was followed by several boys at school. I am pretty sure that Bobby knew her too. I think Bobby knew another Sharon who had died.

Bobby was about ten years old when Mr. Baldridgee took another position at another church, which meant that my number 1 playmate would be moving on. I might never see him again. We did not have a car so that we could go visit to play together. I lost total contact with Bobby for about five years. Bobby was an excellent athlete; we were about the same skill level, I would say. After graduation, Bobby went to Northeastern to become a teacher. Bobby went back to Salina to teach. He developed an excellent baseball program. One year, they won the state tournament. Bobby gave me a call, wanting to know if I could donate some money so that all of the players could have the special ring denoting that they had won state, which is an incredible accomplishment. I gave the baseball program $5,000. Bobby's baseball program had some kids that were drafted. I believe Sharon Holloway had a son, Russell, that reached triple A status playing third base. Mom kept me informed on a weekly basis on how baseball was going.

Bobby presently lives in Oklahoma City, Oklahoma. I will be sending him some photos of us walking in the woods and on the railroad tracks.

We had no video games to play; we were all playing outside. Bobby was the best playmate I ever had.

Mr. Baldridgee baptized Sissy and me. I was twelve years old and Sissy was thirteen years old at the baptism. He also came back to the church to preside over Sissy's marriage. It was so cool that Mr. Baldridgee called her Sissy instead of Mary Elaine. There was a big void in my life when Bobby moved away.

CHAPTER 14

Robert McDonald

Robert and Bobby Baldridge were my earliest playmates growing up. I started playing with Robert when we were about five years old. Robert was my age and in the same grade. Bobby was one year older. He was not an athlete like Bobby Baldridge was. Robert did not have much of a father figure at all. His dad was white, and his mother was full-blooded Cherokee. His father would park on Main Street and take people wherever they wanted to go. He usually was seen taking women, although he would occasionally take men. Many times there was a Cherokee woman who got a ride into town and needed to go home again. Rumor was that he had quite a few Cherokee women friends. Robert's home was on Main Street. We occasionally would watch cartoons on Saturday morning.

In our backyard, there were tall weeds that were about five to six feet tall. There was an abandoned metal building that used to be used by the electric company. There were metal and rocks lying around everywhere. Snakes were frequently seen. We would play Cowboys and Indians almost every day in the summertime. We made bows and arrows and spears from the bodark tree. The electric company had several poles that were elevated by a platform. We played underneath and on top of these poles. We also had a slingshot. We would pick out a target and try hitting it. Robert and I would put cans on the poles and shoot rocks at them with our slingshots. We had gravel roads, so there were plenty of rocks. We became very good with our slingshots. When we would go walking on the rail road tracks, I would always bring my slingshot. I don't know why, but I called this a "beenie flip." We became very accurate throwing knives and spears at the target. Both of us had knives with which we would throw and try to stick a piece of wood or ground. We became very good at doing this. Robert and I played very well together. Dad put up a tent in the backyard, and occasionally, we would spend the night in the tent. Robert had a cousin who lived in Spavinaw named Jeff. His family would occasionally come to visit, usually on a weekend. He was two years older than me and Robert. For some reason, he did not like me. We would occasionally get into fights. It got to a point where I would go home when he came to visit Robert. It also seemed that Robert would turn on me when his cousin was around. He would never do this if it was only me and him.

One Saturday when his cousin was over, he suggested we go play in the metal building. I thought there was something unusual about this. I entered the building first. I turned around and saw both walking slowly toward me. I walked a little ways and turned again; they continued their way toward me. They were pushing me into a corner. His cousin said, "We are going to beat the shit out of you." They were about twenty-five feet away and approaching. When they were about fifteen feet away, I grabbed a rock and threw it as hard as I could at his cousin. The rock was about the size of a baseball. I hit him on the forehead, and he fell unconscious to the ground. He was bleeding profusely.

I saw Robert draw his knife, and he said, "Now I will beat the shit out of you." I knew how good Robert was at throwing his knife. He kept coming closer and closer. As Robert came closer, I begged him not to use his knife; I knew how good we had become at throwing our knives. One of us was about to get seriously hurt. I looked down, looking for another rock. Instead, I found a piece of metal about six by six inches. I grabbed it and threw it at Robert as hard as I could. It landed on his forehead across his eye; it struck on his forehead and cheekbone. Blood was everywhere. He fell to the ground unconscious. I grabbed his knife and ran to the hay house. I really thought I had killed both of them.

After about five minutes, I heard both of them crying loudly. I was about ten years old during this altercation.

The police came from Pryor to talk to me. I told them what had happened. I was afraid I was going to be sent to Vinita, where delinquent boys were sent. If that was going to happen, sending me to Vinita, I had devised a plan to take King, my dog, and catch a train going north. Many times the train would stop just outside of Salina for a while. I had promised King he would never be a stray dog again, so he would have to come with me. I had about a fifty-yard segment of railroad track where I had practiced running and catching the train while it was moving. I would miss my family, but I was not going to be sent to Vinita.

Thank God I had not killed them. They walked home slowly. They were both taken to the hospital. Mrs. McDonald came to the house and told Mom and Dad what happened. I knew I would get a beating. I told Mrs. McDonald what had happened and that Robert was coming at me with his knife. Mom and Dad were worried that they were going to get sued. We were all three lucky. Things could have been a lot worse. That rock could have hit his cousin in the eye or neck. The piece of tin could have hit Robert in the neck, cutting his carotid artery. Robert or I could have been killed if we had fought when he had his knife.

After this, I never played with Robert and I never saw his cousin again. Soon after this, Robert's Mom died, and Robert was sent to Oaks, a Cherokee orphanage. I never saw Robert again. Mom saw Robert occasionally in the store. She said he had a huge scar on his forehead and cheekbone. Thank goodness his eye was not injured.

Robert died at a young age. He had had a hard life. Shortly after everything happened, Robert finally confessed that what I told his mother was true.

CHAPTER 15
The Bodark Tree

The bois d'arc, also spelled and pronounced "bodark"—tree grows forty to sixty-five feet tall. It produces a fruit that is the size of a softball; however, the fruit weighs more. The Osage and the Comanche Native American tribes would travel long distances because they used the limbs for their bows and arrows, an example of how flexible the tree limbs are. The wood is strong and durable. It is not poisonous, but if a horse or cow tried to eat the fruit, an obstruction to the esophagus is possible. In general, livestock will ignore this fruit. The limbs grow up to three to six feet and are very flexible and strong. It is an excellent wood for fences and ship masts.

Usually around September or October, the fruit will eventually fall from the tree to the ground. The essential oil from the fruit, frequently called "hedge apples," has three components that have been identified as repellents. Many people use the fruit as a repellent for spiders, leeches, and mice by placing it underneath the bed. The tree also produces a long thorn that will cause an early response in people with swelling and erythema, redness, and puffiness, if the thorn punctures the skin.

There was a bodark tree just outside of our back door. There was another bodark tree near the road. To my knowledge, the trees are still there and healthy. When I was seven or eight years old, I realized these balls were very useful at Halloween. I was not the only one that realized this; the kids in town knew where to get these hedge apples.

Mom always wanted me to get all of the hedge apples on the ground and bury them. Little did Mom know that I filled two to three different burlap sackfuls for people who went trick-or-treating with me. The people with us would share in our bodark apples. Mom had a huge bamboo stick that she used to knock the fruit to the ground. This did not prevent people from coming by to see if there was any fruit on the ground and to see if they could knock any fruit out of the tree. We used the balls to throw at the houses of teachers we did not like. These apples, if thrown on the roof, would not cause any significant damage. There were two or three teachers we did not like. We threw these apples through the front doors and screens. These hedge apples are, as mentioned above, about the size of a baseball, and they are heavy. They cause a lot of damage when thrown at a door window. Awnings were a favored thing in Salina. I think because Mr. Childress was building houses and he also made awnings. If anyone found these apples in their yard, they accused me of throwing them at the house. They did not realize that there were a lot of other people who wanted these apples.

One person who wanted to be with us at Halloween was Robert Sitzler. I gave him some hedge apples in a burlap sack also.

CHAPTER 16

Metal Box

Dad was working at McDonnell Douglas as a crater/packer. He made boxes that were used to ship parts of airplanes. Dad would cash his checks and put the money in a metal box, which he kept under the bed he slept in. He would occasionally bring home rolls of silver coins and let Sissy and me play with them. He would, at times, take the metal box and count his money. There was about $500 in the box.

When I was in second grade, I would go to school bragging about all the money Dad had. I told everyone that he kept the money in a metal box and that he kept it under his bed. Mom had a job at McClay's grocery store. She would come home every day at noon to make sure everything was okay. One day as she was about ready to put the key in the lock, she noted that the door was slightly open. As she opened the door, she noted Bimbo, our dog, in the corner shaking profusely. Mom, remembering the money under the bed, ran to see if it was still there. Her worst fear was true; it was gone. Mom went back to work and told Mr. McClay what had happened. She then called the police.

They came, taking fingerprints and talking to the neighbors. Nobody, except one person, knew anything. He said he saw a black car parked in front of the house, and there was a man with a hat on standing in the front yard. The fingerprints revealed nothing. For some reason, the sheriff went to talk to a fortune-teller. It was incredible how accurate she was. She said they very well could come again. Dad loaded the 12-gauge shotgun as well as the .22 rifle. Dad taught Mom how to use both guns.

Mom stayed home for two weeks just in case they did come back like the fortune-teller said. They never came back.

It was devastating for Dad to come to grips that we had lost the $500. That was a lot of money for us. The robbers also injured Bimbo, our dog. He had seizures for the rest of his life. After about a year, Mom and Dad had essentially given up on finding out who broke into the house. Nothing was said about the robbery anymore. About three years later, I was playing football with a friend of mine in the churchyard. We were kicking the football and catching it. My friend kicked the ball; it bounced and went under the parsonage. I ran over, and as I was getting the football, much to my surprise, I saw the metal box. I grabbed it and ran home as fast as I could.

Of course it was empty. If it could only talk. The metal box was never used again. I hated myself for doing what I did. I know how much this meant to our family.

I still have the metal box. Every time I look at it, it brings back a lot of sad memories. We will never know who did this. To this day, I blame myself for what happened.

CHAPTER 17
Walking in the Woods

Walking in the woods was a real treat for me and Sissy. We would frequently have one or two of our friends go with us. Furthermore, we would get to go by the huge trash pile, which was at the beginning of the trail down to the railroad tracks and river.

Sissy and I would quite frequently get one or two toys that were thrown away, which was a real treat for us. If we had a friend go with us—Bobby Baldrigee was one of our friends that frequently went with us—we would usually not get anything from the trash pile because we did not want our friends to know that this is where we got some of our toys. The best time to get toys from the trash pile would be January or February when people would throw their old toys away and get new ones. We got our bike there. Dad worked on the bike and got it running pretty good. Sissy and I rode that bicycle for years. The bike lasted for several years. Sissy would get dolls and stove dishes that she could play with. The trash pile was like looking under a Christmas tree. We occasionally took our rod and reel for fishing. This was a new, very good rod and reel from Jeff, GW's stepdad. We would get fifteen to twenty perch and have our fish fry on a Saturday rather than Friday. The perch was very good. It was a very good meal, and there were no bones in the fish. We would usually have fried chicken if we were not able to catch fifteen to twenty perch.

We had to make it back to our house on a Saturday around three o'clock for the football game in the backyard. There would be twenty to twenty-five kids that showed up and wanted to play. It was Dad's football opinion we had to abide by. We usually played until around 8:30 p.m. The Grand Ole Opry was at nine o'clock. Dad, Mom, and I took our places on the couch. Sissy would play jacks on the floor.

Before we went walking in the woods, we would make vanilla ice cream and turn our ice cream maker around to make sure it was thoroughly mixed. We would pack ice around the entire ice maker. We always had hamburgers in the afternoon after football.

As mentioned before, most of the time, we made it back for our weekly football game in the backyard with Dad. We usually played until dark or around 8:30 p.m., which was thirty minutes before the Grand Ole Opry. Mom would occasionally make sassafras tea, and Ed Hornbeck would come over, two to three times a month, to come walking in the woods and to make sassafras tea. Sassafras is a very bitter plant to eat or drink. One has to know when to get it and how to make the tea. Mom was one of a few who knew how to make it such that it would taste good. It is deadly if one doesn't know what to do. I think what has to be done is that it must be cooked and then diluted over and over again. Especially in the fall, they would come to pick sassafras, almost weekly, on a Saturday. Everybody loved sassafras tea.

CHAPTER 18

My Habits

Beginning in the second grade, I started having horrible habits. The first habit was that I would blink my eyes as fast as I could and for as long as I could without stopping.

For instance, church was an excellent time for me to bow my head and blink as much as I could. By the end of the day, my eyes would be red; they would have erythema and swelling of the upper eyelids. Mom would put warm compresses on my eyes for fifteen to twenty minutes, which made them feel much better. She would also put a topical antibiotic on my lids. There was a time when I could stop my blinking for two to three hours, which helped a lot. People would stare at me as if to say "this boy needed help." There was no help other than warm Epsom salts applied to my eyes and eyelids. I could tell that they were improving. Before too long, Ms. Brown gave me a letter to give to my dad or mother. It read, "Mr. and Mrs. Yarborough, your son has a habit of blinking his eyes, and I feel it is hurting his grades. He plays very well with other kids. I suggest you take him to your family physician for further evaluation." Mom made an appointment to see Dr. Cameron, our family physician. He said that habits like this frequently are copied from someone else that the person idolizes. This could be a teacher of his. Mom and Dad discussed this with me. I told them that I had an insatiable urge to blink my eyes and that I did feel that I was getting better. The warm soaks and topical antibiotic were helping a lot. I felt that the ocular anxiety was decreasing. Mom followed me to school the next day. She gave Dr. Cameron's letter to Ms. Brown, my second-grade teacher. Dr. Cameron's letter said that there was nothing wrong with me. Mom looked at Ms. Brown and stated, "I see you have the same problem yourself." They stared at each other for the longest time. Dr. Cameron's letter was also given to Mr. Brown and the grade school principal. He was a very understanding teacher.

Unfortunately, the ocular anxiety gave way to spitting. Again, I could not help myself from spitting. I spit everywhere I went. One embarrassing incident happened when Mom, Sissy, and I went to church on a Sunday night. We were having a church revival. The church was full except for the two bleachers at the front of the church. I had been saving my saliva for quite some time. As we were about to sit on the bleachers, I felt the urge to spit, and I did. The spit went on another lady's head, neck, and back.

She immediately turned around and asked, "What are you doing?" Mom said, "We are so sorry. He has a habit of spitting. He cannot help himself from spitting everywhere." I wanted to get out of church as soon as possible. Dr. Cameron did tell Mom that I should not be spitting so much. The saliva is needed to help digest and absorb our food. My lips became very dry it caused ulceration, redness, and swelling. When I came home from school, Mom would make me drink three to four glasses of water. Mom would also put Vaseline and Neosporin on my lips.

My most unusual habit was that I had to look down at my thumbs every time I played sports. This lasted only a few weeks and was gone. Thank goodness.

The next habit was when I would curl my toes in my shoes all day long. The smell of my shoes and feet was horrendous. Mom would soak my feet with Epsom salts at least one time per day, and if it was possible, two times a day. She would put powder on my feet and in my shoes. The tennis shoes that I was wearing smelled horrible. We had to put them outside on the porch because the smell was so bad. The next day, we went to the secondhand store and got me another pair of shoes. It seemed soaking my feet in Epsom salts helped a lot. After about two weeks, the smell decreased to the point of being nonexistent. There were no lasting effects from this.

The next habit I had was whistling. This lasted two to two and a half months. I would whistle everywhere. I would frequently whistle in church. Mom and I would sit in the back pew. When the whistling got bad, Mom would take me home and then go back to church to get Sissy. Sissy would ask Mom, "What habit does Sonny have at this time?"

Mom replied, "Did you not hear someone whistling in the back of the church? That was Sonny." My only child that had habits was Hope. She would lick her lips until they were extremely dry and ulcerated. She had this habit for two to three months before it resolved. We got her some lip balm to apply to her lips when they were dry.

I had habits probably for sixteen to eighteen months. The only time I got relief from my habits was when I was sleeping. For instance, when in church, Mom would rub my back, and I would relax. At the end of the sermon when the song was sung, I would whistle the song rather than sing it. At the end of the sermon, I was awakened by a fart that the entire congregation heard. What an embarrassing moment! I left the church that day as soon as I could.

My next habit was whittling. I had several knives. I frequently would carry a knife or brass knuckles for protection. Showing these two items would typically result in the assailant moving on. Furthermore, I was very good at throwing the knife and sticking it in something. Robert McDonald and I became very good doing this. That what I was afraid Robert would do is to throw his knife at me when we had the altercation in the dilapidated metal building behind our house. Throwing a rock at his cousin and a piece of metal was bad enough; however, the situation could have been much worse. Furthermore, I had a file that I frequently used to make my knives very sharp. I would whittle during my spare time. Mom would try to keep me as busy as she could. During church, I would bring in a stick of wood and whittle during church service. I would sit in the last pew by myself. If I was left alone, I would whittle the legs of our wooden chairs. I would have cuts extensively on both hands. This habit lasted six to eight weeks thank goodness, because I was destructive with my knives.

Sissy, Dad, Me, and Bobby walking in the woods.

Sissy and Me holding up our Christmas tree. A very unusual April snow.

Me and Sissy with our duck, Webbie. The window next to the board leaning against the house is the window where the Old Man shot a deer slug, missing me by six inches. The tree in the background is the infamous Bodark tree.

Me, Sissy, and Mom standing beside a rocking chair that Dad made.

Me and Sissy going to first day of school. I am in first grade, Sissy in second grade. Note the gravel road and old auto. Also note the ditches on the side of the road. These I scoured around town for pop bottles for money, especially around the Fourth of July.

Grand River.

Me, standing in front of our house with a squirrel I shot. The areas without grass are the areas Sissy and I rode our bicycle around the house. We could not ride on the roads.

Sissy, Me hugging one of my dogs, Dad and then Bobby on the banks of Grand River.

Sissy, Me, Bobby, and Mom sitting in front of "Bears Mailbox" which was a big hole in the tree. We would put letters in the hole, which was addressed to Mr. Bear. We also put our letters to Santa Claus in there every year.

Me and Dwayne Sasser getting ready for a baseball game.

Mom, Me, and Sissy working in the garden. Note the chicken house in the background to the right. Our toilet, connected to the chicken house immediately to the left. The metal building with part of the roof torn off is where I just about killed Robert McDonald and his cousin.

Bobby, Me, Sissy, and Mom. Bobby and I with a cane pole. I had a lot of worms in a can. Grand River is to the left, down a very steep trail. These are the railroad tracks that I walked on with my dogs, numerous times. These railroad tracks gave me solace when I needed it. When I looked down the tracks, I knew there had to be something better down those tracks. Note the steep bluffs to the right. When the lake came in, it covered the railroad tracks between 15 to 20 feet deep. These are the bluffs that Phillip and I dove off of. One had to take a running dive or jump, otherwise you would hit the bluff below.

Me, Sissy, and Dad in our garden.

Bobby, Me, and Sissy watching Webbie take a bath. Note the tent and campfire in the background. Our church is the building to the right with three large windows.

Me to the left, Bobby in the middle, and Sissy to the right. Mom in the background: walking in the woods.

Sissy and me standing on the porch.

Left to Right: Bobby holding a rod and reel, Mom holding a gun, Sissy, Me holding three squirrels I killed. The man with the tackle box, rod and reel, and cigarette in his mouth is Ed Hornbeck. The man to his right is his father. Ed was married to Dad's sister Ann. He was a very nice gentleman. He was a firefighter.

Me, Mom, Sissy, sitting on a log. The church is in the background. There is a white building to the right of the church, the space in between these two buildings is where Bobby and I would play baseball and football. Basketball was played in our backyard.

My mother, her mother, Grandma Dobbs, Lillie Mae (Mom's sister and Grandma Dobbs' other child). Front Row: Me, Sissy, Bobby, Lige. Note the tent in the background.

Our graduation class. Me in the middle with Mike Haley to my left and Clarence Kingfisher to my right.

Bennie Erwin, Mike Haley, Me, and Warren Whiteday.

Sissy, Me, and Dad on our porch.

Sissy, Me, and Mom.

Me with one of my dogs.

Me with my very first dog. You can read the story in the chapter My Dogs.

Sissy, Me, and Mom. Our church and parsonage to the left.

The old home place. The house that built me.

CHAPTER 19

The Old Man Next Door

There was a basketball goal in our backyard. Many times, there would be other kids that would come by to play also. If there were enough kids, we would form two teams and play games. Sometimes there would be four to five kids on each team. Behind our backyard was a telephone company. There would be four to five of these men that would come over and play with us also. We would choose up sides and play. We would frequently play until dark. It really increased my basketball skills playing like this. Normally, we would get quite noisy. Mom would look out the back door frequently as she prepared supper.

There was a house just next door where an old man lived. He was creepy and emaciated. He was blind in his right eye. He always had a hat on. There was not much conversation with him. He would occasionally call me and Sissy over to have watermelon with him. But we would not have watermelon or any other food with him. He always had a Schlitz beer can everywhere. He talked about gold and silver in the hills outside of Salina. He was psychotic. We would frequently see him with a pick and shovel going to the hills. He did not have an automobile. I seldom saw somebody in a car stop at his house, or even stop in front of his house. Neither Sissy nor I ever asked him what his name was. To us, he was just the old man next door.

Occasionally when he was out of sight, I would break into his house to see what he had. It was unkempt everywhere. His icebox was basically empty. He had a wooden stove for heating. His kitchen was empty. His bedroom had a bed that was dirty and smelled. On the wall he had two rifles, two shotguns, a .22 rifle, and a pistol.

We kids would occasionally get loud while we played basketball or football. As Mom was looking out the back door one evening, she saw the old man aiming a rifle toward the kids playing basketball. She immediately ran out the back door, hollering at him to put down the rifle. The old man went back in the house quickly. Mom broke up our game of basketball, and everyone went home. The next afternoon, I went out to shoot some hoops without experiencing a problem. Mom and Dad called the police on that next day too. The police came and talked with him. He denied that he pointed a rifle at us while we were playing. After Mom saw him that one time, she frequently would look out the back door if there was a group of kids playing out there. Mom observed him pointing a rifle at us playing basketball on three different occasions.

One Saturday night, Dad heard a loud sound that woke him up. It appeared to be coming from the backyard. He did get up and grabbed his shotgun and looked out the back door. He saw nothing. I was asleep in the back bedroom of the house. Mom and Dad had recently converted the storage area to a bedroom that I could sleep in. I did not hear anything. The next morning, Dad went out into the backyard and saw that there was something that had hit the house. He started poking the area and he saw a deer slug that hit an area that would have been six inches from where I was sleeping if it had gone through the wall into the house. The trajectory pointed to the old man next door. Dad called the police. The police did come and looked at where the slug hit. They went and talked with the old man and brought him over to look at the point of impact, a futile attempt to warn him against this happening again. A deer slug, going through the window screen, six inches to the right would have hit me in the head or chest while I was sleeping. Death would have happened instantly.

What was I to do? The old man had aimed his rifle at me three different times as observed by Mom. Now he aimed his shotgun at me while I was sleeping and missed me by six inches, a shot that could have killed me instantaneously. After much deliberation, I felt that the best thing was to go and get all of his guns. Someone was going to get hurt or possibly killed. I asked Sissy if she would help me. I got two pairs of gloves, one for Sissy and one for me. Sometimes when he went to dig for gold, he took a shovel, a pick, and a rifle; but this time he was just carrying a pick and shovel. I was outside shooting baskets. He said nothing to me. I called for Sissy. Thank goodness she did not have any friends over at that time. I got the gloves, and I told her how we were going to do this. I waited until he was out of sight and thirty minutes beyond that. Thank goodness his house was unlocked, so I could enter his house. I got the two rifles and gave them to Sissy; they were loaded. I did not know if Sissy could carry them or not. I did not want to take a risk. I told her to carry them with the barrel pointed up. We were going to have to make two trips. These were too heavy for Sissy. She carried a rifle and a handgun. We had to make sure that there was nobody outside and that the old man was not coming back early. All of his guns were loaded. I took a rifle and a shotgun. We carried them home and put them on the kitchen floor. There was nobody around, and the old man was not seen. We went back and entered the house through the same door. I looked through the house for any more guns. I took as much ammunition as I could. We took the shotgun and the .22 rifle and another pistol. I thought that we had got all of his guns. Mom looked at them and agreed that taking his guns had to be done. I told Mom I was going to put them underneath the floor in the closet where Dad kept some of his money. They were all impressive guns. He had taken good care of them.

The next day, as I was playing basketball, he came over and wanted to talk with me. He said that somebody broke into his house and got all of his guns. I told him I did not observe anyone around his house when I was outside playing basketball. There could have been someone while I was out there. He appeared distraught. He said he was going to call the police. I told him I would let him know if there was anybody going in and out of his house while he was gone. The disturbing thing about this was he told me that he would kill anyone breaking into his house.

Despite all of this, we continued to play basketball in the backyard. I felt we had gotten all of his guns in his house. Nobody knew anything about this except me, Sissy, and Mom. Mom continued to look out the back door as she prepared supper. The old man did call the police. The police did come and interview me one afternoon while we were playing basketball. We still had to be very careful because he could have gone to a friend's house or bought another rifle and shot us dead. The rifle that he had had was a very powerful one.

One day, as the old man went to dig for gold and silver, I put on my gloves and broke into his house again. Again, just to make sure he did not have any more guns. Sissy was keeping watch outside of his house. I looked extensively throughout his house, looking for any more guns. I could find none. I walked away feeling confident that he did not have any more guns. Again, I got as much ammunition as I could.

One Saturday morning four months later, his house caught fire and burned to the ground. The old man was never to be heard from or seen again. We kids thought that the old man was burned to death on that Saturday morning. The old man was a chain-smoker. His cigarette smoking certainly could have precipitated the fire and his death. One day, while playing basketball, a person told me that the old man had syphilis, which certainly seemed possible given his situational responses.

CHAPTER 20

Baseball Camp

Richard Crawford asked me if I could go to a good baseball camp in Branson, Missouri. If we went right away, the camp would not interfere with school. I asked Mom and Dad if I could go; they agreed. Camp was divided into three, three-week segments.

Unfortunately, we started camp one week into the third segment. Why Richard asked me, I do not know. The name of the camp was Show Me Baseball Camp. Mom and Dad saw me play several times. They knew I was an accomplished catcher. They knew I would be better if I went to the camp.

Mr. and Mrs. Crawford took us to a baseball store in Tulsa. This, I thought, was incredible. I had a good catcher's glove but not a bat. Dad gave me enough money with which to buy a bat. With a hug and kiss from Mom and only a hug from Dad, we were off to the camp. The other thing I wanted was to see a skyscraper; I wanted very much to see the skyscraper of a bank building, which was approximately thirty stories tall. The baseball store was fantastic. There were several bats to pick from. I settled on a thirty-three-inch Louisville slugger with a narrow handle.

It took about three hours to get there. There was no interstate at that time. When we arrived, we checked in and the rules and regulations were gone over. One rule was that we were not allowed to play catch or any form of baseball outside of regulation play. If we did, the coaching staff would make us run, do push-ups, and so on. It made you never do the repercussions again. There was also a curfew at night to get to bed.

There was a counselor in each building. There were three to four kids that were sons of baseball players on the Kansas City Royals team. It was difficult to get to sleep at night; I finally did.

One day, about 6:00 a.m., Ernie came into the dorm area and yelled, "Is there a catcher in here?" I jumped down from the top bunk and told Ernie that I was a catcher. There was not another catcher in my building. He told me to cover up my white legs; I would get them very burned in the hot sun. I slipped into baseball pants, and I grabbed my catcher's mitt. Ernie was an excellent pitcher with the New York Yankees. The weather was excellent at that time. Everybody else went back to sleep for another hour.

Ernie started slow until he could tell I was a good catcher. He started to throw hard. He had to be throwing upper eighties to low nineties. I prayed that he would not throw one into the dirt. I had no protection. He did throw a few in the dirt. I had no protection from the balls that were thrown into the dirt. Fortunately, I was able to catch them before they hit me in the wrong place. There were two other catchers but not of my caliber. There were traveling teams that came every day except Sunday. They were from Missouri, Illinois, Kansas, and Oklahoma. We would work on the basics of baseball in the morning and play a game in the afternoon. I was definitely the best catcher there. I started the games, and after five or six innings, the other catchers would play. It was a good baseball camp. Richard and I very much enjoyed the camp.

I was going to get the best catcher award as given by the coaches; however, Richard and I had started the second week of a session that disqualified me from getting the award, unfortunately. Both of us felt that we markedly improved our baseball skills. One afternoon, Mom and Dad called me from the pay phone on Main Street. I told them that it was a good camp and that I was learning a lot. I told them I needed to go three weeks rather than two. They said okay. I told them the food was good and plentiful. I had put on about fifteen pounds, and I was learning to swim. There was an excellent swimming pool. I was not a good swimmer initially. There was a coach who helped me learn to swim. I swam every day. I could tell that I was getting better as far as swimming was concerned.

CHAPTER 21

Locust Grove Baseball

Clarence Kingfisher and I played summer baseball for two summers in Salina. I played twice as many games because I played catcher for the older team too. I had developed into a very strong and good catcher. Clarence was the ace pitcher for the younger team. He could throw hard and had an excellent changeup and curveball. Why we did not have summer baseball beyond these two summers, I do not know. I was, as well as Clarence, saddened that we were not playing summer baseball.

One Saturday night, as we were getting ready to listen to the *Grand Ole Opry,* I could hear what seemed to be cars parking in front and to the side of the house. The shades were drawn, and the front door was closed. I could hear people walking on the porch and talking. The next thing I heard was a knock. I went to open the door. They wanted to know if my dad was there. Dad went to the porch. I could not hear what they were talking about. Dad was there for about an hour. I could not think of something bad I had done; I had not been in any recent fights. I did not think I was in trouble with the law. Mom and I listened to the *Grand Ole Opry.* Finally, I could not hear any more talking. Dad came back in the house and said that they wanted me to play summer baseball with them. Locust Grove said they had watched me play baseball several times. They knew that there were several other teams that were going to be after me. And indeed, there were three other teams.

We had played Locust Grove a year ago, and I was very impressed with their team. They had a good left-handed pitcher that could throw very hard. Unfortunately, when his father found out about the coach drafting a player from Salina, he would not allow his son to play on the team. I offered to forfeit being on the Locust Grove team. The coach would not hear any of that. What a team we would have had if his dad had not interfered with his son's baseball playing. At the end of the summer baseball, the year before, I went to baseball camp for three weeks; this was in Missouri. My baseball skills had markedly improved even more after the camp. There is more about baseball camp in another chapter.

Dad said, "They wanted you to begin soon."

I stated, "In three days, I will be ready." There would be practice every day except game day and Sunday. We would practice on Saturday if need be. I had mentioned to the coach that we should get Clarence Kingfisher. He said that would be great. Clarence and I were saddened about not playing summer baseball, but now, our prayers had been answered.

Clarence, like me, was wanting to play summer baseball. When I got home, I called Clarence from a pay phone on Main Street. We did not have a phone at home. Clarence was ecstatic. Now, we had two very good pitchers. We were in a very good conference. Locust Grove and Salina were very competitive when they played each other. They really did not like each other. This did not matter to Clarence and me. We were playing baseball, and that was all that mattered. The people in Locust Grove were expecting this team to go far. The townspeople knew that the team had picked up a catcher and a pitcher from Salina. After the first game, they did not realize how good a team they had. I dominated hitting, and Clarence pitched an excellent game. He had increased his velocity as compared with the year before. His curveball and changeup were excellent. He usually got three to four days' rest in between games. The attendance was incredible. Not only did the players' moms and dads attend, but it got around the town that Locust Grove had an excellent baseball team and they were fun to watch. Midway through the season, Clarence and I spotted who else but Sam

Baker attending. It had been a year since we had seen Sam. After the game, it was wonderful to talk with Sam. As I was staring at the floor, I could hear Sam saying, "Sonny, you play catcher." Playing catcher with that funny glove that I had never seen before, I had developed into an excellent baseball player as evidenced by several teams wanting me to play for them. I was a little anxious meeting the players. Everybody welcomed us. I think they were all thankful that I was playing with them rather than with another team. We practiced every day, and we developed into a very good team.

People began to see how important Clarence and I were to the team. Several games were won because of Clarence's pitching and my hitting. We played two to three games per week. The other two pitchers on the team were decent. Also, midway through the season, we began to play as an excellent team. All of the people from Locust Grove, as well as the players, were very appreciative that we played on their team.

It came down to one game as to who was going to win the conference and advance to the regionals. We had not lost a game. The team we would have to play was Colcord. It was a home game for us. They had a very good team. Their pitching was excellent. We were tied going into the last inning. There were two outs, and the count was 3–2. The pitcher threw me a fastball down the middle of the plate. I connected, and I could tell it was hit on the "sweet spot" on the bat. It went sailing over the center fielder's head. There was no fence. I was not going to take any chances, and I ran as fast as I could. Who was coaching third but my Dad? When I reached home, the center fielder had not caught up to the ball. I was tackled at home plate, and everyone jumped on. That was an incredible feeling. We were going to the regionals!

I got a hug and a handshake from the parents and from fans of Locust Grove's team who attended the game. The parents had been incredibly supportive of me and Clarence all season, even though I did not know them. I could tell that Dad was proud of what I had done. I did not know what Dad was thinking when the ball was sailing over the center fielder for a home run. I wonder if he thought about all those days that we played catch in the front yard when I was a little boy. I wonder about the time at the supper table when I told them I played catcher when I was not supposed to. I never discussed this with Mom and Dad; I just savored the moment. The parents knew that we would not be going to the regionals if it were not for me and Clarence. It was a couple of hours before the coach, Dad, I, and Clarence could get away. The parents told us that was the longest home run ever hit on that field. The ride back to Salina was quiet. I think everybody was savoring the moment. The game we had just played was very intense. I think everybody was tired both emotionally and physically. Nobody in Locust Grove had predicted this when we had arrived to play for the team.

Mom met us at the porch. The coach told us he would get back in touch with us the next day. Hopefully, we would have a few days off to rest. We had been playing a game or practicing every day for a long time. Dad told Mom what had happened during the game and that I had hit a homer to win the game. He told her how the players mobbed and tackled me at home plate. He told her how appreciative the people had been. He told her that we were heading to the regionals. Mom said, "Come here, Sonny." She then gave me the biggest hug I'd ever had. She told me that she loved me and that she was very proud of me. I told Mom that Clarence had pitched a helluva game. Mom had prepared an incredible supper. I asked Mom if Clarence could eat with us. She replied, "Absolutely." We ate everything Mom had prepared. Soon, after supper, Clarence's parents came and got him. I told them that Clarence's pitching had won the game and that we were going to the regionals. I told Clarence that if he could come by the next day, we could play some catch, and we would also find out whom we were playing against and where.

I think, more than any other sport, baseball players have the most superstitions that they have to follow. For instance, Justin Verlander does everything in threes. My bat was a thirty-three-inch Louisville wooden bat. I got this when we went to Tulsa with Richard Crawford. The bat had not been broken. It had been with me ever since I had this indescribable urge to put my bat into the compost pile, buried in the rotting food, leaves, grass, and waste from chickens, horses, and cows. The more odiferous it was, the better. I told Mom and Dad that if they saw my bat in the compost pile, they should just leave it alone; and if it was uncovered, they should cover it back up. Nobody else knew about this. Mom said that they understood. They did not seem too surprised, especially with all of the weird habits they had to put up with from me when I was a younger boy.

The next day, we found out whom we were going to play against. We were playing the team on a neutral field in Tulsa. The game was in four days. At least this would give Clarence some rest. We did hitting and fielding every day. Clarence did some hitting, and that was it. On game day, we got to the field early. I was relaxed, and so was Clarence. There were an incredible number of people there from Locust Grove at the game. It is interesting that nobody from Salina except Mom and Dad knew we were playing baseball with Locust Grove and that we were a very important part of the team. If Salina did know, they would probably want the other team to win. Salina and Locust Grove do not like each other in sports. Both my mom and dad went to the first regionals game.

The game was a very close game. Clarence had his fastball, curve, and changeup working very well for him. He threw a four hitter, two of which were thrown out at second base. In the fifth inning, the bases were loaded; I got a hit in the gap between right field and center field, three runs scored. The score was 3–0, Locust Grove on top at the end of the game. I knew that every game was going to be close and that we would not win if we made mistakes. I could tell the team was very anxious. They were ready to play anybody. I warned them not to get overconfident. The next game was two days away. Clarence had never pitched with two days' rest.

There was very little conversation going back home. I think all from Locust Grove and the players were mentally and physically fatigued.

That is not to say that everybody felt we could win the state. It was a healthy anxiety. Mom and Dad came to the game.

At both regional games, I was concerned about Clarence having two days' rest, although I did not mention that to him. Both Clarence and I were mentally and physically tired. We went to bed early. Clarence told me he would be ready to go with two days' rest.

The next regional game was to be played in Tulsa, about a seventy-mile drive. The only thing we knew about the other team is that they were a good hitting team. The first thing I did when we got home was to bury my bat in the compost pile. I certainly did not want Clarence to know about this superstition of mine. For supper that night, we had fried chicken, pinto beans, and fresh salad from the garden.

The next day, Clarence came to the house; he said he felt good and his arm was not sore or stiff. We decided to run and then throw some when we got back. Running felt good. Clarence threw the ball and had no pain or stiffness. Clarence ate with us that afternoon. Very little was said about the game the next day.

The next day, we arrived to the field early. Again, Clarence told me his arm felt good. When I warmed him up, I did not want him to throw very many pitches. Again, the attendance from Locust Grove was incredible. Clarence pitched a strong three innings of no-hit ball. In the fourth inning, I could tell his velocity was not as strong. We went to mainly curveball and changeup. They scored four runs that inning. We came back and scored three runs—I hit a home run with two on. The score going into the last inning was 6–4, Locust Grove. In the last inning, the first batter up singled. I went to the mound to hopefully relax Clarence. The player who singled was thrown out trying to steal second. I went to the mound to talk to Clarence again. I told him, "Just two outs and we advance to the state." I told him we were winning with his curveball and changeup. I told Clarence if I call for a fastball, I wanted it to be high. I told him the ump was calling low balls strikes also. The next batter flied out to center field almost over the fence. The next batter was the seventh hitter. I went back to the mound. I told

Clarence that this was his last batter of the game. Indeed it was. He flied out to left field. Everybody tackled Clarence; he had pitched a helluva game. Everybody from Locust Grove was shouting, "State, state, state!" In the beginning, nobody would have thought this team would get to go to state. We had a good team, and we got some breaks along the way. Clarence's parents were at this game. The parents of the players as well as the other people from Locust Grove were in disbelief. We celebrated for a couple of hours and headed home.

The first thing I did when I got home was to bury my bat in the compost pile. Again, Mom had prepared a hearty meal. I was so tired that I went to bed around nine o'clock. Clarence came over the next day, and we threw the ball for around thirty minutes. Clarence said his arm was a little sore and stiff. I told him if he had some peas or beans in the freezer, he should put a bag on his shoulder and his elbow.

The first game of the state tournament was to be played in Tulsa but at a different field. The game was scheduled three days from the day we were playing catch. I did nothing except shoot some baskets the next day. I had previously gone over some stretching exercises for Clarence. He stated that he was doing them, religiously. I told Clarence that we did not need to throw anymore. I told him if he wanted to come over and hang around some, that would be good, but otherwise, I would see him at the game. I articulated to Clarence that I was very relaxed. No matter what happened in the state tournament, this had been an incredible summer of baseball. I told him what I thought: "You and I had markedly improved over the summer." He was in agreement.

Clarence and his parents came by the house to follow us to the field in Tulsa. Clarence rode with me and the coach. Mom and Dad rode with Clarence's parents. We got to the field early. I did not want Clarence to throw much. He said his arm was not sore but was a little stiff. He threw until his arm was feeling good. This team was good. There were an incredible number of people from Locust Grove. Clarence pitched three innings of no-hit baseball. Their pitching was the best we had seen. The fourth inning, I could tell his velocity had decreased. We went to mainly curveball and changeup. They scored four runs that inning. We came back and scored three runs. The fifth inning, I hit a home run with two on. Clarence got tired in the sixth inning. He had to be taken out. This was the first time he had to be taken out. Our pitching beyond Clarence was not great. In the sixth inning, they scored three runs and won the game. Everybody was very saddened; however, nobody would have predicted a season like ours. The parents had planned a party for Saturday night. Both Clarence and I were going to attend. Clarence and I took a long walk together. We were very thankful that we were able to play summer baseball. We felt that we were better players because of this. Clarence was very thankful that I suggested to the coach that we get Clarence for his excellent pitching.

Everybody was quiet on the way back home. Clarence rode with his parents. We all were going to the party Saturday night. The loss did not lessen the pride that everybody had for this team. We learned that the team that beat us won the state championship.

I did not have to bury my bat in the compost pile. Instead, I retired that bat. It was a thirty-three-inch Louisville slugger, narrow handle. I wish I had that bat. It would bring back a lot of memories.

Saturday night was the party at Locust Grove for the baseball team season. My mom and dad went; however, Clarence's parents did not go. It was an incredible party. It was true that if it was not for Clarence and me, this team would not have made it past Colcord. However, most games were certainly a team effort. There was also some luck along the way. I wonder about the kid whose dad did not allow him to play because there were two kids from Salina playing on the team (the kid missed out on a lot of very competitive baseball.) I did say, time and time again, that it was a team effort. I could not believe that the girls wanted an autograph from Clarence and me. Everybody treated Mom and Dad with a lot of appreciation. I think they had a good time also at the party and were surprised with the comments the Locust Grove parents made. The food was great. We were there for about three hours.

The girls were wanting a phone number from me. I told them we did not have a phone. They were all very surprised.

On the way back to Salina, Dad was asking all types of questions. When we arrived home, the coach got out of the car and gave Clarence and me a big, big hug. He was very appreciative, obviously. He thanked us and told us he would keep in touch.

The next summer, Locust Grove and Salina did not have summer baseball. We did not have a phone or automobile. This was very surprising to everybody. We stayed in touch only when Salina played Locust Grove. It always brought back incredible memories when we played with them.

I did not play summer baseball again. Instead, I spent my summers cutting wood, hauling hay, and digging ditches. I have not seen Clarence for fifty years. I wanted to talk with him about his memories of Locust Grove baseball and what it meant to both of us. I am sure he had a lot of fond memories. I was extremely saddened to find out that Clarence died a year ago, 2018.

About a week later, as Roger and I were coming back from a hard, hot day of chopping wood, I could see Dad and the Locust Grove coach standing on the porch.

As he gave me the plaque, he congratulated me on being chosen "first team, all state catcher;" and so was Clarence as pitcher. Coach told me that there was going to be a traveling team that was going to be contacting me, "they want you to be their catcher. This team is the best in the state of Oklahoma."

Indeed, they did contact me. They begged me to join their team. They traveled all over Oklahoma, Texas, Kansas, and Arkansas. I begged Dad to let me join this team. Instead, he wanted me to chop wood, hall hay, and dig ditches. This was again devastating to me. We did not have a phone for communication, no automobile for transportation, and no extra money. This is what happens when you live in poverty.

For a long time after this I would wonder what would have happened if I would have played with this traveling team. Would I have been drafted, would I have received a scholarship to a major university with an excellent baseball program, and so on. Indeed, this has haunted me for a long time. This I will never know, the answers to these questions.

CHAPTER 22

Robert Sitsler

Robert was a boy with cognitive differences who was in the fifth grade. Robert was about three years older than most of the students in his class. For about three years, Robert had been held back. A significant thing about Robert was that when he grinned, his teeth were green. I don't know if he ever brushed his teeth. Another thing was that he was 6'5" tall. He got into a lot of fights because of this. He carried brass knuckles as well as a knife to protect himself. He never knew when a carful of boys would pull up beside him and beat him. He would run to disperse them, and then he could easily beat the crap out of one or two boys, especially with his brass knuckles. Robert was left-handed and very strong. In fighting, he had a good left-handed punch.

One place he loved was coming over to play with the rest of us, usually basketball. He knew I would not stand for any fighting. Mom was not that far way either, fixing supper. I did not tolerate jokes on him also. I think that Robert, most of the time, had a lot of fun playing basketball with us. I encouraged him to go out for the basketball team. He never did it.

I am sure Robert was smoking and drinking alcohol at that young age. There was really no one to tell him not to do it.

Robert and I had a few fights but none like this one. We were playing basketball together. I was teasing him, and for some reason, he snapped and came after me with his knife. I knew how dangerous Robert was, especially with his knife. He started swinging his knife with his left arm. He cut my coat with his knife. I was able to kick him in his groin with my right leg. He fell to the ground in pain. Shortly thereafter, I felt something on my left hand; it was blood. I ran to the kitchen hollering for Mom. As I was taking my coat off, I started having pain in my arm near the shoulder. I was bleeding profusely. We applied pressure over the cut. This seemed to stop the bleeding for the moment. I hollered to Robert to get the hell out of our yard, "if you are going to act like this, you will never play with us again." Little did we know that there are three big arteries that supply blood to the upper extremities, called brachiocephalic. If he had cut the brachiocephalic artery I would have bled to death. After about twenty to thirty minutes, there was no more bleeding. Taking off my shirt, I could see a cut about three inches long about four inches superior to the elbow. To this day, I can see the scar. We continued putting pressure on my arm. After about twenty to thirty minutes, there was no more bleeding, thank goodness.

Robert lived with his parents. They too had cognitive difficulties. I met them a few times when Robert came to the house to play basketball or football. I was Robert's friend. He probably never took a bath. When he would begin to get hot, he had body odor (BO), very strong. His parents were morbidly obese also. They had several guns in the house. Guns were not what Robert needed to get a hold of. Came to find out I was able to do my work and help him with his, especially reading. Occasionally, at recess he liked to read to me. His grades improved some. I think he could hardly read before. I went to teachers and told them that he needed help with his reading. Whether they had no interest in this or there was no money allocated to a student who had problems reading. When reading was better, improved, his grades improved. I am sure his parents did not care whether he graduated year after year or not. Robert went walking in the woods with us a couple of times. His grades were improving, and he was having a good time in school. In the seventh grade, we were at different campuses. He did not have me to tutor him. He had no one to teach him about reading. He did not come to school anymore midway through the school year. He joined one of the gangs in town. There were three or four gangs in town. He was shot and killed on Main Street. There were a couple of times where Robert prevented me from getting into dangerous situations. We miss him. God bless him.

CHAPTER 23

My Dogs

Pooch was a very good dog. He was not mean at all. I don't know where Mom and Dad got him, more than likely he was a stray dog. This is the way most people got their dogs at that time. That is how I got my first dog too, which was in front of McClay's grocery store. I told Mom and Dad that I was going to go and get me a dog, and that's exactly what I did. There is a picture of me bringing him home from McClay's grocery store.

Pooch was terribly afraid of storms, especially those with a lot of thunder and lightning. He did not tolerate this very well at all. If the storms were really bad, he would be in the cellar with us. Usually in my or Mom's lap. We could feel him shivering all over, which decreased if he was in my lap or Mom's lap. We rubbed his body as well as his head. If there was potential for a bad storm, other people would come to the cellar. All of the people were welcome. Dad would sit at the bottom of the stairs; other men would sit at the upper part of the stairs. If something bad was happening, we would close the door to the cellar. The men would stand. People would also bring their dogs if they were really afraid of storms. Everyone got along very well without any problems whatsoever.

One Saturday, I decided I wanted a dog. I was about six years old. There were plenty of stray dogs all over town. One place in particular was at McClay's grocery. Furthermore, Mom was working there at that time. There were usually several stray dogs at McClay's because people would feed them as they shopped for their groceries. I went in and asked Mr. McClay if he had any bones or scraps. He replied that they were over in the box and that I could have all of them. There were ten dogs in total, and I took all of them behind the store and fed them. They thoroughly enjoyed the bones and scraps. Several of the dogs had mange, but not bad. After being with the dogs for a couple of hours, I decided on a beagle-like dog who was white with black spots. He did not have a name, and he was very friendly to me. I picked him up and carried him home. We have a picture of me, with a hat on, carrying the dog. I named him Spot. He reminded me of BB, a dog that Brett and Ashleigh have. I had made a hay house with a large fenced-in area. This was the perfect place for my dogs. I spent quite a bit of time with him so he would get used to me and not run off. He was fed very well. He loved to hunt. That was probably the beagle in him. We always took him when we went walking in the woods. He loved to swim in the river. Many times we would get four to five squirrels. We would skin them, and Mom would fry the legs. Dad and I were the only ones that ate them. The dogs got the scraps.

Monroe, a friend of mine, was the dog catcher in town. A better term for him was "the dog killer." He would shoot them with his 12-gauge single-shot shotgun. If a dog was hanging around someone's house, the person would talk to Monroe, and he would take care of it. When he would shoot a dog close by, I would hear a loud bang and then a god-awful cry for twenty to thirty seconds.

One day, as we were plowing, I asked Monroe why he killed dogs. His reply was, "Because I get paid for this." I asked him if he would please take me the next time he was going to "take care" of a dog. He stated that he would. I will never forget the situation when he took me. It was a mutt that was starving to death. The dog had horrible mange. I brought some bologna with me. He was easy to catch. I placed a rope around his neck and lifted him into the wagon. He ate the bologna in no time. As I jumped up into the wagon, he lay down beside me as close as he could get. I got him into the hay house without a problem. The other dogs seemed to welcome him. It was almost as if they remembered being in the same situation at one time. I spent the next two nights sleeping with my dogs just to make sure there was no fighting.

The next day, I covered the new dog with motor oil, followed with an Ivory soap bath. I did this for three straight days. He, the man at the gas station on Main Street (the place where Mom and I went to get our treats after our naps), gave me two gallons of motor oil without any charge. I went to McClay's store and got bones with meat on them as well. I also had some bologna, which I got at McClay's store. I asked Monroe if he could pay me a dollar per day. He agreed to do this. That helped a lot. I named the mutt Bullet, because he dodged Monroe's bullet. The next day, I took him to the ditch and covered him with motor oil again. I massaged his body very well. He really enjoyed that. The motor oil was followed by an Ivory soap bath. I did this three different times. After the third time, the scratching was about gone, and his hair was growing back. He was putting on weight and doing good. I followed this protocol with every dog I got. It worked very well. Why the used motor oil got rid of the mange, I do not know. I took Monroe to the hay house and showed him the dog I had rehabbed. He could not believe his eyes.

When I thought that the dogs were out of danger, I would give Lillie Mae three or four of them. She loved the dogs, plus they served as protection for her. She would frequently let the dogs inside, especially in cold weather. The dogs had plenty to eat, and they had 250-plus acres to roam around on. One of the dogs became an incredible cattle dog. We named her Shepherd.

There was an incident that happened with a puppy of mine. I should have kept him on a rope for a while. As the puppy was crossing the road, a man ran over my puppy, killing him. The driver should have seen him. He had plenty of time to stop. I was furious. The man was the brother of our next-door neighbor. It took me a day before I could settle down in my mind and think of what to do to this SOB. The next day, the opportunity presented itself. The brother parked on our side of the road. He came to see his sister. I remember I had used an ax the day before. I went to the back of the house and got the ax. I proceeded to knock out the glass and the lights. I made sure there were some major dents in his car also. I went and sat on the porch, waiting for him to come to me. If he had come into my yard, there would have been serious consequences.

One afternoon, after supper, Dad and I were playing catch in the front yard. I could see a stray dog was walking down the road in front of our house. I fell in love with that dog at first sight. I told Dad, let's have a time-out just for a minute. The dog was emaciated and had terrible mange. I think he fell in love with me, and after rubbing his head for quite a while, I told him, "Let's go." He followed me to the back of the house. We had fried chicken for supper. There was some left, so I gave the remainder to him. I did get in trouble because of this. I also gave him a bowl of Purina. He loved that also. I put him in the hay house, and Dad and I finished playing catch. I spent the night in the hay house without any incident. The next day, I followed the motor oil and Ivory soap bath protocol. He loved the attention. He was getting better after a week. He was growing hair and gaining weight. I named him King.

There was only one usable bedroom in the house. Mom and Dad took that, and Sissy slept on the couch and I slept on the floor in front of the potbellied stove. We burned either coal or wood, whichever was cheaper for the winter. It was my job to bring in enough coal or wood for the night. I had to look at the wood to make sure there were no black widow spiders. They were frequently in the wood. If I woke up, I had to make sure that there was a fire going or hot coals present.

Eventually, when King was rid of the mange, I would bring him in the house and he would sleep with me on the floor. I promised King that he would never be a stray dog again. He seemed to know and understand what I had said.

In the years to come, King and I had many good times. We also had some close calls. Either way, he was always there for me and me for him. I was with King when he died. We did not have a vet where I could put him to sleep. Instead, I comforted him the best that I could. I kept telling him that I loved him over and over. I am sure he had a hard life until he met me. His life thereafter was depicted like his name, King. I kept my promise to him. He was never a stray dog again. At times, he was the only friend I had. At times, it seemed he was the only one that loved me. It was hard to come to terms with the fact that he would never sleep with me on the floor with my arms wrapped around him again. We had been through so much together. I buried him behind the cellar house, where the rest of my dogs were buried.

I cried and cried especially at night for a long time. I missed him so much. Mom comforted me as best as she could. She knew I was having a hard time accepting the death of King. As time went on, accepting his death seemed to get easier. I still miss him immensely. I hope that when I get to heaven, I will be able to see all of my dogs I helped have a better life, and that I will be able to sleep next to King again. There will be more about King throughout the book.

For a time, I guess, I was the dog catcher in Salina. They would tell me about dogs they wanted to get rid of. I would get the dog and do my routine of motor oil and good nutrition. There were probably forty-plus dogs that I was able to rehab. I made sure these dogs got good homes. It was hard to give any of the dogs away. However, with good nutrition and attention, they grew to love their new homes. I would go and see them occasionally. Remembering the circumstances they were in when I got them, I would cry with joy that I was able to give them a good home.

Every time that I got a beating at home or a paddling at school, I felt shame, unloved, and violated. After each incident, I would go to the railroad tracks and river, trying to clear my head as to what had just happened. I personally found solace walking down the railroad tracks and staring and wondering if there was a better life somewhere down those tracks. As a young boy, I had done several things that could have sent me to a home for delinquent boys. This was before my dog, King, came into my life. There was about fifty yards of the track that I had marked off that I could run and catch a boxcar while the train was moving. I had practiced this time and time again. The hard part was jumping off the boxcar, not hopping onto the boxcar.

I was determined that I was not going to be sent to a home for delinquent boys. I would miss my family immensely, but I was not going to be sent to this delinquent home. When King came into my life, I promised him that he would never be a stray dog again. The train did quite frequently stop for a while, which gave me the opportunity to lift King into a boxcar.

One Saturday in early October, King, Bullet, and I were walking north on the railroad track. We met a hobo on the tracks. He was waiting for the train going north. I asked him what the next town going north was. He said it was Big Cabin. I asked him how long it took to get there. He replied, "About three hours." He asked, "Don't you think you are too young to be hopping a boxcar?" I replied, "No, not at all." He asked me what I was doing with the big knife and the shotgun, and I replied, "Hunting."

In mid-November, I decided to hop a boxcar going north. I knew that the train stopped in Salina for a few hours. There was no way I could put King on the boxcar while it was moving. I was about seven years old at this time. I lifted King into the boxcar. As I climbed aboard, I could see that there were four hobos at the opposite end of the boxcar. I would say they were in their thirties, all had long hair and long beards, and all appeared unkempt. I looked at them but did not acknowledge them in any other way. I made sure that they saw my shotgun and my long sharp knife. My shotgun was loaded and ready to use if somebody tried to harm me.

As I sat down on the floor of the boxcar, King got as close to me as he could. He began to growl. I grabbed his mouth and kissed his nose. I told King that everything was okay. I started rubbing his chest, and he settled down. Only two of the hobos asked me questions; however, all eyes were fixated on me and King. They wanted to know my name. I gave them a fictitious name (Ken). They wanted to know my last name. I replied that I was not going to give them that information. With these two items, my shotgun and long knife, they would have been fools to try something. Finally, the train began to move. After about thirty minutes, one of the hobos had to pee. He went to the opposite door from me and peed.

The ride to Big Cabin seemed like it took hours upon hours to get there. I was so tired I closed one eye. I had one hand on the shotgun and the other one on the knife, ready to be used if needed. I prayed to God that everything would be okay. I could feel the train slowing down. After about fifteen minutes, it came to a stop. I asked the hobos if this was Big Cabin. They replied yes. I asked them which train goes back to Salina. They replied it was usually the middle train, but that I had better ask the conductor which train goes back to Salina. I waited about fifteen minutes after the hobos exited the boxcar.

Looking out the opposite boxcar door, I could see a large restaurant called Big Cabin Café. King and I were so hungry and thirsty. We had been traveling for many hours without eating or drinking. As we entered the café, I told King to stay close to me on my left side. We went to the last booth. There was nobody around. I laid my shotgun and knife on the opposite seat out of sight. One of the waitresses saw me enter the café with a dog. She immediately told me the dogs are not allowed in the café. I begged the waitress to allow me to keep King in the café. I told her that I did not have a collar and leash for my dog. I told her I could not afford anything like this. I would be afraid to have him stay outside because somebody might harm or steal him. I told her that I had only one dollar and asked, "How many cheeseburgers will that buy?" She replied, "Four cheeseburgers." I told her that was what we would like. She left to place the order.

I lay my head on the table and closed my eyes. It felt so good to do that. Before too long, I felt somebody touching my shoulder. I raised my head; it was the waitress. She said, "Look what I found." It was a very nice collar and leash. She said she found it in the lost and found. I could not believe I was getting a very impressive collar and leash for King. He looked very handsome in his new collar. The waitress wanted to know my name. I replied, "Sonny," and I asked her what her name was. She replied, "Betty." I thanked her profusely for the collar and leash. She asked me what I wanted to drink, and I replied, "Water for both of us." She asked me why I was traveling alone. I told her I might be in trouble with the law, and that is all I want to say about this.

Before too long, she came back with the hamburgers and the water. She brought a bowl for King to drink out of. I divided the hamburgers into four quadrants, two for me and two for King. They were so good. King began to salivate profusely. Betty came back when we were almost done. I thanked her for her kindness, and I told her I hope to meet her again in the future. I grabbed my gun, knife, and the leash. This felt so different walking King with a leash. I gave Betty a dollar and a half. I felt so ashamed that I could not give her a bigger tip. She was a wonderful waitress, but even more, she was a wonderful person. I prayed to God to honor and reward her for what she had done for me.

As I walked out the door my, next task was to find the train heading to Salina. I prayed to God that he would lead us home safely. I went to the train that was running. I climbed up on the locomotive and asked the conductor if this was a train going to Salina. He replied, "Yes." I asked him if the train was going to stop in Salina for a short time. He replied, "Yes." I asked him when the train was leaving. He replied, "In about thirty minutes." I picked the second boxcar to board. I was hoping that the train would stop where I could see the lights of Salina. I didn't think I could have made it home walking through the woods. I had no light. I now recognized the importance of carrying a flashlight with me on my next endeavor like this. I lifted King into the boxcar. I was glad to find out there were no hobos in the boxcar. It was pitch dark. I could see nothing. King got as close to me as he could. We were both very tired. We both took a nap after the train began to move. Time began to move fast. Before too long, we were stopped in Salina. I did not have to walk long before I was home. I fixed my bed on the floor, and King and I went to sleep. But before going to sleep, I prayed and thanked God for keeping us from harm.

CHAPTER 24

Halloween

Trick or treat was so much fun. It was held on October 31 at night. When Sissy and I were small, Mom would always take us trick-or-treating. We would get lots of candy, which would last us three to four days. Mom would always check our sacks when we came home before we could have them. Dad did not dress up but would hand out the candy while we were trick-or-treating. We would have lots of fun. We would have lots of kids come to our house at Halloween. Mom always decorated very nicely. Mom would decorate the porch and dress up like a witch. The little kids always liked coming to our house. She did this until one of the preachers at church gave a sermon on Halloween, stating, "If you decorate or dress up like a Halloween figure, you are idolizing the devil." It was inappropriate to say something like that. Mom did this for the kids. Mom would never idolize the devil. Mom never dressed up like a witch after that. She curtailed her decorating of the porch. Sissy and I usually wore a mask that Mom would buy for us in Pryor. My favorite thing to dress up as was a ghost. We got all types of candy. My favorite was a peanut patty. Mom checked the candy for razor blades.

As we got older, Sissy and I were able to do trick-or-treating by ourselves. At about age ten or eleven, we were able to go with friends. Bobby Baldridgee and Robert McDonald went with me; Sissy had her own friends to go trick-or-treating with. This is when the tricking began. A favorite thing for the high school boys to do was to go around town turning over toilets and doing other acts of vandalism. Our toilet was connected to the chicken house, so they could not turn our toilet over. They would also steal younger kids' candy. The teachers in school that they did not like were particularly picked to be vandalized.

There was a bodark tree in our backyard. The tree produced a fruit that was about the size of a softball. The fruit would fall to the ground in October. The older boys would come by and steal them and throw them at cars and houses. We would try to pick up the ones on the ground and throw them away. Through the years, I went with several different boys trick-or-treating. There would usually be four to five of us going together.

My job, before Halloween, was to gather up all of the balls that were on the ground. Little did Mom know that we boys were going to use them. I would get about three burlap sacks halfway filled and put the balls in them. We would throw them at teachers' houses we did not like. One teacher in particular was Ms. Allen. This is the one that taught nothing but music. Furthermore, she did not give out any candy, and her house was always dark. When I was diagnosed with peptic ulcer disease, Dr. Cameron, our family physician, wanted me to take a medicine on a scheduled basis. This was to be taken around one o'clock. At that time, I would go and ask her for my medicine. She hated this as much as I hated to ask her for it. She would sometimes throw it to me, and sometimes it would fall to the floor. How embarrassing was it when I had to crawl on the floor to get my medicine. I hated her as a teacher. I would bombard her house with the hedge apples, as well as her windows and front door. We would break into the schoolhouse and get two to three cases of soda. I would climb up to where the bell was and tie the rope so it was unusable. We would turn our desk in the study hall and put chairs on top of the tables. We would tie the two front doors together so people could not enter the school through the front doors. The superintendent had an idea of who did this but could not prove it. He usually called several boys into his office and asked if any of us did this. We all said no. He told us if anybody is caught, there would be serious consequences. We never got caught. Other teachers' houses were bombarded with the hedge apples also. Fireworks were also set off around town, especially Roman candles.

One Halloween, Dwayne Sasser, a friend of mine, sat out on his horse for trick or treat. Robert Sitzler went with us. He would walk along beside us. I got the three of us quite a few hedge apples and put them into burlap sacks. We tied them together and hung them over his horse. After we bombarded a few teachers' houses, especially Ms. Allen's, we went to the high school and did our usual vandalism there. It was getting late, and Dwayne asked, "What else do you want to do?"

I said, "Let's try to ride Master across the porch where the new girl in town lives." We were in the seventh grade, and her mom was a new teacher in school.

Dwayne replied, "Let's do it." We approached the house cautiously. I got off of the horse and got the reins. He would not go. I kept pulling on the reins. I slapped his butt and jumped up on the porch. He let out a very loud sound as I jumped back on. Things were getting loud. Lights came on in the house, and I could see someone coming down the stairs as I jumped back on Master. My boot went through the screen door and glass window. I must have jammed in the lock because he had a hard time opening the door. Once I got back on the horse, I slapped his butt as hard as I could, and he jumped off the porch without hurting himself. We rode as fast as we could.

Eventually, her brother got the door opened and yelled, "You SOBs [sons of a bitches]," as he shot the gun in our direction. His aim was way too high for the bullet to hit us. We were too far into the darkness for him to see who we were. We rode to the boat landing, where we hid the horse. We both waded into the water. We were ready to swim to the other side if someone came. After about thirty minutes, we felt that we were safe to go. It was hot and the water felt good. We rode home without anybody seeing us. When I got home, no one was awake. I fixed my bed on the floor and fell asleep. The next day at school, Dwayne, Robert, and I were called into the principal's office.

Dwayne Sasser and I went trick-or-treating for about three years straight. We went trick-or-treating on his horse during that three-year period of time. As previously noted, we rode the horse over the porch of one of our teachers. She was the mother of a popular girl in our class. We were in seventh grade. I guess we were seeking attention. Every year, there were people who would get together and talk about the most unusual things that had happened on Halloween. Riding a horse over the porch without any consequences like getting caught by teachers or police was the most unusual for that year.

Every year, there was a lot of damage to Mrs. Allen's front door and two side windows. Dwayne, Robert, and I were called to the principal's office and asked if we threw all of the balls through the front door and windows. I replied, "I threw three balls, but they all landed on the roof." There was no glass broken. The other two threw two to three balls also. Again, these landed on the roof. There had to be someone else running through the yard picking up these apples. I guess Mr. Jones, the principal, did not buy our story. He said he was going to have to give us twenty slaps with a wooden paddle. I went first. God, did that hurt. It did not need to hurt that much. I went to the restroom, sat on one of the stools, and cried for thirty minutes. The next day, I showed Mom my butt; she was appalled at what she saw. She walked to the school and met with Mr. Jones. She told him that she was appalled at what she saw, swelling and bruising. She told him that he was going to get in trouble if he continued to paddle in such a manner.

He said, "Your concern is noted."

Mom said, "See, you people do not look at what you're doing to these areas. Someone is going to sue you for producing this. These areas have extensive bruising and swelling. Furthermore, paddling is not going to deter this from happening again. There are different ways of punishing kids rather than causing extensive swelling and bruising. We will not be suing you, but you better have a damn good reason for a paddling in the future."

Mrs. Stuart's daughter, whom every boy in school wanted to "go with," laughed at us and called us stupid. We were. The twenty slaps were bordering on too much. It was the most painful punishment I had ever had at school. A beating with the bodark limbs is much worse because one hurts all over, especially the back.

Looking back, I can see how teachers and schools got sued for use of the paddle. Paddling did not make Dwayne and me stellar boys. And indeed, this was not the last paddling we got. We were shunned by our class for quite some time.

CHAPTER 25

My Worst Beating

One October Saturday morning, Robert McDonald and I were sitting on the porch talking about the robbery of our house. I was about seven years old at that time. Dad, who was sitting in the front room, heard us talking. He came out and proceeded to ask Robert about what he knew about the robbery. The most incriminating question was about me going to school when I bragged about the amount of money we had in a metal box that Dad kept under the bed. Why Dad did not put the money in the bank, we will never know. Dad told Robert to go home and told me to come inside. I had no idea what was going to happen; it did not look good. Prior to this, discipline consisted of a slap or a hit by the belt and the like. Dad went to the bodark tree in the backyard near the house. He got three long bodark limbs. The limbs also had thorns on them. Dad came back into the kitchen. He told me not to run, and then the beating began. The bodark limbs were the worst. With one hit across my back, I fell to the floor withering in pain. It seemed as if the beating lasted for hours. I know what I had done, bragging about the money, was inconceivable and painful to the whole family. It took Dad many years to save the $500 in the metal box. However, did the beatings make things better somehow? Other than Dad taking out his aggression on me, I don't know.

I lay on the floor, crying, trying to make sense of what had just happened. He used the entire set of three limbs. I don't think Dad knew how badly the bodark limbs injured my back. While on the floor, Mom came over and raised my shirt and said, "Oh my god."

I eventually got up and crawled out the back door to the hay house, which was about seventy feet away. I was hurting all over but especially on my back. It was soothing to be with my dogs; I knew they loved me. I was also very disappointed in myself. King came and licked the tears from my face. I eventually fell asleep crying. I awoke probably a couple of hours later feeling very hurt and unloved. The hay house and the dogs gave me tranquility. I grabbed my bowie knife and a large butcher knife, which I stole from Mom. I kept it between the bales of hay so that it would be safe and not harm anybody, unless I needed to and because it would be almost impossible to find. (I wonder what would have happened if Robert McDonald and I had gotten into a real fight regarding his knife when he was coming at me to harm me. The endorphins, a morphine-type compound, are released into the bloodstream when there is severe pain. I am sure that my endorphins had been at a very high concentration.)

I decided to walk to the railroad track and then to the river. The entrance to the bluff, railroad tracks, and river is now the boat landing. I told King he needed to go with me. Bullet really wanted to go with me also. I let Bullet out of the hay house. There was no hesitation. We walked past the trash pile where Sissy and I would look for toys that we as a family could not afford. We finally made it to the railroad tracks. We looked down the tracks, and I wondered, if I caught the train and headed north, surely, things would be better than what they are now. King would definitely have to go with me because I promised King he would never be a stray dog again.

I did not want to go back home. It was early October, and we had some cool nights. I did not think snakes would be a problem. We took the long trail to Grand River. The water was swift and deep. I had to keep telling myself to not go close to any water except for a drink because I could not swim. I made my way down the bank, walking cautiously through thick brush. I had to get to a place where I thought it would be impossible for someone to find me. I finally made it to a clearing where there was a huge boulder with enough room for me, King, and Bullet to get underneath. We were so hungry, and there were blackberries. They tasted very good. Even King liked them; Bullet did not. I decided to make three spears for myself. I made one end very, very sharp. I was very accurate in throwing spears. I then proceeded to clear out the area underneath the big boulder. I thought I saw leaves moving. Yes! It was a big water moccasin. I trapped him with my spear and cut his head off with my butcher knife.

As much as Dad and I drank the river water, it is a wonder we did not get a waterborne disease like giardiasis. Plus, there was a laundromat not too far away that put all of their waste water in the river. This is the same laundromat that Mom took our clothes for washing.

I did not want King or Bullet to get involved with the snake. I saved the leaves to cover myself up. I got one more drink of the river water.

I climbed up on the huge boulder. I sat there for a while looking out over the river, wondering if I would be missed. There really wasn't much Mom or Dad could do. At that particular time, there was no police in town. I turned my head to the right, and what did I see? A huge wasp nest, teeming with wasps. I slowly turned my head, looking straight ahead. The nest was probably twelve by twelve inches in size and about a foot away from me. I slowly got off the boulder the same way that I had gotten on the boulder. That was a very close call. I think I was very lucky that I did not get stung by multiple wasps.

Bullet was also an incredible dog. He was just about dead when I got him. Bullet was underneath a house. He was so emaciated and full of mange. I wrapped a rope around his chest, and Monroe pulled him out from underneath the house. We put him on Monroe's trailer and took him to my home.

It was time for some rest. I sat on a rock, crying and staring at the river, wondering if I would be missed and if they really loved me. How could they love someone and beat someone like this? King came over and put his head on my lap as if to say, "Everything will be okay." Despite the endorphin high, I was still hurting a lot. It was just about dark and I was very tired. I was also getting cold. I got as far underneath the big rock as I could. I covered myself with as many leaves as I could. Whether this helped or not, I do not know. I had both Bullet and King lying down beside me. King came and lay down beside my abdomen and chest. Both were very warm. This helped a lot. I put my arm around him, hugging him as tightly as I could. I rubbed Bullet's neck. I could tell that he was getting sleepy. I prayed to God that everything would be okay. I tried not to think what the consequences of running away were going to be. Would they welcome me with open arms, or would I get a few slaps? Surely, to God, there would not be a repeat of today. I was hurting all over, especially my back.

I finally fell asleep, crying. Sometime during the night, I was awakened by rustling in the leaves. It was so dark I couldn't see anything or anybody. I grabbed the big butcher knife, ready to use it if need be. I put my hand over King's mouth and rubbed Bullet's neck, whispering, "Everything is going to be okay," over and over. Eventually, whatever disturbed the leaves moved on.

I awoke at daybreak thirsty, cold, and very hungry. I am sure King was also. We went up to the railroad tracks and started walking north. We met a hobo, who asked me what I was doing on the tracks so early. I told him that I had spent the night on the riverbank. He was very surprised and told me to be careful. He was eating some bread. I asked him if he had any extra. He gave me four pieces of his bread. And I asked him if it would be okay if I gave my dogs a piece. He stated, "I do not care." King and Bullet gobbled this up rapidly. He said he was waiting for the train heading north. He asked me what I was doing with the knives. I told him they were for protection. I walked farther north before turning south to go home. I walked very slowly. I thanked the hobo for the bread, and we went our separate ways. I dreaded going home.

I walked slowly back home. I could see from a block away that Mom and Dad were working in the garden. I hid my knives and spears in the tin barn near our house. When Mom saw me, she came running and gave me a hug. "Where did you go? And why did you do this?" she asked.

"I don't know, Mom." I did not want to get into a discussion about feeling unloved and worthless and so on. She asked me if I was hungry. I said, "Very." She had fried chicken, potatoes, salad, veggies from the garden, and plenty of it. King and Bullet had their food to eat as well as some of mine. King, Bullet, and I ate everything there was. Nothing was left.

It was about six o'clock. Dad continued to work in the garden. After supper, I went to the living room and lay on the couch. My back was hurting from the previous beating. There was still quite a lot of pain. I heard Dad come in the back door. I could see he had two bodark limbs in hand. He immediately started beating me with them again. He repeated, "You don't do this again," over and over.

Mom came rushing into the living room from the porch, hollering, "Dad, stop this!" repetitively. She grabbed him, but it was too late. The beating was over. This renewed the pain in my back.

Mom and Dad went to the porch to sit. It was about six-thirty. I lay on the couch for a while. Although I was hurting all over, I wanted to go and shoot some baskets. Now was a perfect time to go and get the spears and knives that I had and put them in the hay house, where they could not be seen by anybody. All my dogs were happy to see me. When it got dark, I went and sat on the porch. Sissy came out, and we talked for quite some time.

Mom and Dad went to bed early that night. I made my bed on the floor, got King and Bullet, and went to bed with them. I fell asleep immediately. The next morning, Mom woke me and Sissy for school. I hated school. I was learning absolutely nothing. There were two thorns stuck in my back that Mom had to remove. They were causing me a lot of pain. I went to the sink to wash my face and hands. As I looked into the mirror, the dark areas on my face were not dirt; they were bruises.

I walked to school that morning not talking to anyone. When I walked into the classroom, my teacher pulled me aside and asked me what happened. I asked her, "What do you mean?"

She responded, "Your face is bruised." I told her I was in a fight. She then sent me to the principal's office. Mr. Jones was a fair man. He asked me what happened. I told him I was in a fight. He wanted to know if it happened on school grounds. I told him, "No."

"Who were you fighting with?" I told him I was not going to tell him.

He said, "Okay, go back to your class and don't let this happen again." I left. These beatings were new in my life. Being hit with one of those bodark limbs resulted in horrendous, lasting pain, especially if it was a thorn that was embedded in the skin. If I needed to be disciplined, I was whipped with bodark tree limbs. I know I was a hard kid to control. This was the only form of discipline my dad knew how to use to control me. I do not know if he was disciplined in this manner or not. We never talked about it.

One weekend, I had done something that Dad did not approve of. He thought I needed to be disciplined because of this. Dad came into the kitchen with three bodark tree limbs. I was about fourteen years of age. He called me into the living room, where he was waiting with the three limbs in his hand. He was about ready to hit me. I backed up and told him that I was tired of these beatings and that I would not take any more of them. I told him I would take him down and he would get hurt. I was tall and also very, very strong, and he knew it. I had been in several fights, and I had not lost many. Dad stood there for the longest time, looking at me in disbelief with the three bodark limbs in his hand. I stared at him as if I would take action if he came at me. His initial facial expression showed anger. Who was I to tell him what discipline was going to be? His expression changed from anger to almost crying, as if he was very sorry for the past beatings. He walked away and put the three limbs high on the kitchen counter. Those three limbs were never used.

I did a lot of soul-searching over those years of beatings. One good thing that came out of this was that I promised God and myself that if he ever gave me any children, I would not hit them or switch them in any manner, ever. God has given me and my wife, Linda, five wonderful children, and I have kept that promise to God and myself.

CHAPTER 26

Philip, My Cousin

Philip was a cousin of mine, the son of Goldie, my father's half sister. Philip never had a father figure. His real father worked for Edison Electrical Company in California. He was climbing a pole when his safety belt tore, and he fell to his death. I do not remember my uncle at all. Philip's mother received a large amount of money. She remarried; this man was not a father figure to Philip at all. It was thought more than likely that this marriage between Goldie and this man was that the man married Goldie because of the injury money. He never worked. For a period of about ten years, Goldie and her husband, Gene, would drive back to Oklahoma. They would drop Philip off, and they would proceed to go to Arkansas, where there were other kinfolk. I was about seven or eight when this started. Usually, Philip's stay was seven to ten days. Philip had blond hair; he was about 6'1" and had a good build. He was a very handsome boy, but he had a major problem with stuttering. His personality made up for his stuttering and saved him from being bullied. They always came back for the Fourth of July; fireworks were illegal in California but not in Oklahoma. We loved popping TNTs, cherry bombs, Roman candles, and so on. We would see who could hold a firecracker in their hand the longest. A firecracker going off in a person's hand, but not for long. It is a numbing feeling. We didn't do this with a TNT or cherry bomb. There would have been a definite hand injury.

Shortly before the Fourth, I would go around town looking for pop bottles to sell so I could have enough money for the fireworks. There was a carnival that would come to town July 1–4. Salina also had a very good fireworks display on the Fourth. We could see the display very well from our backyard. Most of Dad's half sisters and their families would also come back for the Fourth. Philip was the only cousin I spent a lot of time with. On the Fourth, we would go to the carnival in the afternoon and come back home, where we would have a big picnic in our backyard. Most of Dad's half sisters would come and enjoy the Fourth. It was a great time. Lillie Mae, Lige, and Grandma would also be there. Every kid would have a bag of fireworks to set off. Dad would occasionally set off a string of fireworks. This was his favorite way to pop the fireworks. When Philp and I went to the carnival, we had to be ready for gangs that might jump us. We both carried a knife and one brass knuckle. Pryor police were there, but they would be of no help. In the early years, Dad's mom and stepdad would also come back from California. His stepdad loved to fish. He would go to Grand River and fish for perch, bass, and catfish.

There would occasionally be a big party after the Fourth at Grandma's house. Jeff loved to fish; he was very good at it. I will never forget that there was a big container that held Coke, Pepsi, and so on, plus Schlitz beer. That was the first time I ever saw Schlitz beer, or any beer for that matter. We would usually spend the night at Grandma's house, where we would sleep on the screen porch. During this time, I could hear either wolves or coyotes. There was a creek called Wolf Creek.

One day when I was twelve, Philip and I decided to ride the Ferris wheel. As we got in line, there was a girl that turned around and looked at me. I thought she was the prettiest girl I had ever seen. We stared at each other before I finally introduced myself. She was with her younger cousin. I asked her if I could ride the Ferris wheel with her. She looked at my knife that I had with me, and she asked me why I had the knife. I responded, "For protection." I gave my knife to Philip. Her name was Betty Haley. After giving my knife to Philip, I asked if I could ride the Ferris wheel with her. She said yes. She was from Brownsville, Texas. She said her family came up to visit her grandma. I knew Grandma

Haley fairly well. We would pass her house every time we went to the river and railroad tracks hunting. I asked Betty if I could see her again and she said okay. As we left the carnival, she introduced me to her cousin, Mike Haley. Little did I know he would become one of my best buddies.

The next day, Philip and I went to Grandma Haley's on our way to swim and visited both Betty and Mike for a few hours. We stayed in touch with letters, and every year we would hang out with each other when they came to visit Grandma Haley. Two to three years later, Mike moved to Salina, and I kept in touch with Betty through Mike. When I entered Oklahoma State, the letters became few and far between. She called me one week and wanted to know why I hadn't been writing her. I told her I had been very busy with my studies and basketball. I told her I would try to be better at writing her. I didn't see a reason to stay in touch. About a year later, I saw her at Mike's funeral. We went on a long walk and talked for a few hours. She was going to college in Texas. We talked about Mike and how devastating losing Mike had been for me. I was going to miss him. I told Betty about the incident on the football field where we hit each other, resulting in the pathologic fracture of his collarbone. Shortly thereafter, he was found to have testicular cancer. When we left each other, I told her I would try to do a better job keeping in touch with her. I was very concentrated on my studies at Oklahoma State.

I remember the run to the lake with Mike, which was about five miles, when it did not seem he had the stamina that he usually had. I remember when Mike and I were getting ready for football regionals. Mike said he was going to run over me. It was a very hard hit, which resulted in the fracture of his clavicle. The evaluation for his collarbone resulted in the finding of his testicular cancer.

Week after week, I could see the water encroaching upon the land. Some people loved this. Real estate value increased. Boaters and other people were ready to start fishing. The lake gave Philip and me new territory to explore. We learned to ski, but most of all, we loved to swim and dive. When Mike Haley moved to Oklahoma, he went everywhere Philip and I went. We went to the lake every day. The boat landing was the perfect place for us to go. This was the entrance to the river and railroad tracks that I had visited many times as a young boy. It was where the junk pile had been, where Sissy and I would get toys to play with. The boat landing was about thirty feet deep, and we could easily swim across.

Somehow, Mike had heard that one of our classmates, Sammy Hesser, was taking his girlfriend somewhere on the other side of the boat landing. We swam across the boat landing. We didn't have any shoes to wear. There were many sharp rocks. We walked for quite some time. Eventually, we found them lying on a blanket. We started throwing rocks around them. Sammy soon saw us. Sammy was not very popular in our school. He did not play any sports and basically kept to himself. We introduced ourselves to his girlfriend and asked if we could hang around for a while. We were on the bluffs on the other side of the lake. The water was thirty to thirty-five feet down. There was a gradual slope to the bluff. Soon, I saw Philip run by me and take a dive off of the bluff without looking. I soon took a run and dove off of the bluff. It was great. I swam over close to the bluff down about fifteen feet, where I found small gravel that covered the railroad tracks. The good times and the bad times I had on the tracks came back to haunt me. I grabbed a handful of the small gravel and kept it. We spent the afternoon diving off of the bluff and swimming.

Mike was not as much of a risk-taker as Philip and I were; however, Mike Haley had a good time swimming. Sammy and his girlfriend stayed for a couple of hours before leaving. On the way back to the boat landing, Philp decided he was going to jump out of a tree that hung out over Lake Hudson. Philip climbed the tree and jumped, and immediately I saw blood. When he made it to the surface, he said he hit his back. He swam to the boat landing entrance; Mike and I followed. When we got to the bank on the opposite side and climbed out of the water, I saw that Philip had some fairly deep cuts on his back. His back was bleeding fairly profusely. When we got home, we had to tell Mom what we were doing. We were not to go to the lake anyway. She had told us that earlier in the morning. We cleaned and dressed Philip's back daily; it did not get infected. His back was healing. We did not do any more swimming. Furthermore, Philip's ride to California was within a day. The cuts left severe scarring on his back.

One summer when Philip was dropped off, we had a day or two swimming at the boat landing and diving off the bluff. We decided we needed something more. Philip, Mike, and I decided to go to the bridge, on the Fourth of July, leading to Locust Grove and dive off of it. Mike had a car and we headed there. Philip and I got on the bridge, and before I knew it, Philip was climbing over the railings and dove into the water. He came up, telling me to move over some because he hit the bottom. I climbed over the railing, moved down some, and dove into the water. It felt great! We spent a couple of hours swimming and diving when Philip decided he wanted to go to the big bridge and dive off of it. Both Mike and I told him he was crazy. Philip talked Mike into taking him over there. We all looked at how far down it was. Mike and I said, "Holy shit." Philip decided he was going to dive. He went without knowing how deep the water was. Furthermore, this area of water was known to harbor some very large catfish; hitting these, one would more than likely be dead. When he came up, he hollered, "Move over some. I hit bottom with my foot." I moved toward the center of the bridge, deciding to give it a try. I dove instead of jumping; timing was important because a belly flop would cause great injury. Too far forward would hurt the back. To protect my head, I made a big fist with my hands and away I went. It was a long way down but it felt good. I thought I hit bottom with my foot as I turned to surface, but I was not sure.

It was the Fourth of July and Salina was very busy. Philip and I would wave to the people driving over the bridge and then dive. Before too long, the police came and we had to leave. Looking back on this, it was good that we left before somebody got killed. We left and went to the carnival for a while, and then home to get ready for the big party at the house.

One summer, when Philip came back from California, he did not know that Roger Klinger and I were chopping wood every day. Dad had bought forty acres and wanted it cleared. Roger needed a job to pay for the very nice Thunderbird, which he eventually bought. Neither of us was very good at swinging the ax. It was in July and it was hot and humid. Temperatures were over a hundred degrees, but it did not matter how hot it was; we were out chopping wood every day.

One day, Philp had to take a dump. There were no toilets to go to. I looked up and saw a sturdy limb above me. I told Philip to climb the tree, go out on the specific limb, and take his dump at that place. He followed through with Roger and me laughing so hard we cried. We watched as the crap flew. Philip climbed down, we had no toilet paper. I told Philip the only thing he could do was try to use leaves. Philip did. Roger and I stayed away from him for the rest of the day. After cutting wood all day, Philip and I would go to the boat landing for a couple of hours and then meet up with Mike and go to visit some girls.

Between my sophomore and junior year at Oklahoma State, I decided to be an orderly at Ventura County Hospital in Ventura, California. I was in premed at Oklahoma State. I had not seen Philip for a couple of years, and we were looking forward to seeing each other. As an orderly, one just performed general care of the patients. I liked the job. There was another guy there who had already been accepted to Loma Linda Medical School. I initially stayed with Patty, my cousin, in her apartment.

Flying to LA was fun. It was my first plane ride. The pilot pointed out different places, such as the Grand Canyon. It was incredible. Soon, Philip got his own apartment, and I moved in with him. Philip had no job. He stayed home and drank beer and smoked all day long. He was taking some classes at a local community college. He wanted to be a cop. After work, we would go and hang out with some of his friends.

There were two interns at the hospital. I idolized them. I wanted to be just like them. It was good to be away from the stress of college for a while. Philip and I would exercise almost daily. I put on about twenty pounds. During college, I usually lost twenty-five to thirty pounds despite eating three good meals a day.

I moved in with Philip after a couple of weeks with Patty. The job was going well. I learned a lot. Philip suggested I could take off a couple of weeks before I returned to Oklahoma, and he would show me California. I did take off. Philip had a white Chevrolet. He said we would drive to Tijuana, Mexico. I had heard nothing but bad things about Tijuana. We left Ventura, California, early one morning. We made it to the Mexican border around 3:00 p.m. It took a while to cross the border into Mexico. Thank goodness we were not searched. Philip had a sticker on his glove compartment that said "Cops Suck" and a large knife inside the compartment. Philip stated that we could not get into a fight because if we were arrested, we would never get out of jail. Tijuana was a hellhole.

There were tents everywhere with a road right down the middle. We were walking, and soon there were two women that grabbed us and pulled us to the center of the tent. We started dancing with them. Before long, there were two guys that came into the tent and grabbed Philip. I saw it happen out of the corner of my eye. I ran and jumped his captors, and we finally got them to the ground. I was heading toward the door when there was another boy who thought he was going to jump me. I grabbed him and threw him into the instruments, and the music stopped. I heard Philip holler, "Let's get the fuck outta here." We ran down the road as fast as we could. Occasionally, we would hide behind a tent just to make sure no police were coming. That was a very close call. All I could think of was that I did not want to stay in jail for a long time in Tijuana. We finally found our car. We jumped inside and took off. It was around one in the morning when we got to the Mexican border. We were both exhausted. When we reached San Diego, we decided to pull over and park on the side of the interstate to get some sleep, which was a stupid move. We finally found a place we thought would be safe. We fell asleep immediately.

About daybreak, there was a tap on my window. I awoke and looked out, and to my dismay, it was the police. They wanted to know what we were doing there. We told them that we had been to Tijuana late the night before and we were very tired. They told us to get out of the car. We were frisked, but they didn't find anything. They then started searching the car. They read the sticker "Police Suck," which did not make the police happy. They opened the gun compartment and found the big knife. The sticker and the knife made one of the police very mad. Philip told them it was for protection. I thought we were going to jail. Philip did a good job of telling the police that he was going to college to be a police officer. They finally let us go. Thank goodness there was nothing else in the car.

I had just finished my sophomore year in college, 1970, when Philip and I were headed to San Francisco. I knew about all of the turmoil at Berkeley. We got off the interstate and parked on a hill. I asked Philip where we were. He replied, "You will see." Before too long, I could see the street sign that said Haight Ashbury street.

I said, "You got to be shitting me." As I turned the corner to walk down the street, all I saw were motorcycles and everybody was stoned. People were lying on the curb and in the street, sleeping, and some seemed to be overdosed on illicit drugs. There were no cars on this street. We walked into the shops; there was nothing but drug paraphernalia and drugs. This was difficult to understand, especially for a boy from Oklahoma. We stayed there for a few hours and then went to Berkeley.

Hippies were everywhere. It was a beautiful campus. We struck up a conversation with one of the hippies. We got an earful about peace, love, no war. We then went to People's Park. Hearing about it, I thought it was going to be something special. I was unimpressed. All it was, was a field with a bunch of hippies running around. It was getting late. We decided to get a bite to eat and to get to bed early. We finally made it to Oakland, where the Black Panther Party was in an uproar. We saw a Nabisco plant up the road, where we thought we would park in the parking lot. We thought we would be safe there. We still had the big knife. We parked and fell asleep.

The back seat was very uncomfortable, especially with my long legs. Within an hour, I heard a tap on my window. He wanted to know what we were doing there. We told him we had been driving all day and we were tired. He said, "You boys know this is Black Panther territory?" We said, yes, we did. He said, "I think you boys will be safe." He suggested that we should keep the keys in the ignition just in case we needed to make a fast getaway. We finally got back to sleep, and we were up at daybreak.

At daybreak we left, ready to go to Northern California. We took Highway 1 up the coast. It was a beautiful drive. We did not stop until we reached the redwoods. They were beautiful and majestic. We found a park on the way back, where we safely spent the night. The next day, we made it back to the apartment. We left and went back to Fillmore to spend some time with the rest of Philip's family. Philip never paid a deposit or any rent. He left the keys and a note on the table saying, "Thanks." Sissy flew out to visit us also. We stayed another week and then flew back to Oklahoma to get ready for college.

I was pledging FarmHouse Fraternity, and I knew it was going to be rough, but I was ready. I learned a lot about the world that summer. That was the year when we landed on the moon. I felt that Philip and I were lucky that we did not get into serious trouble and that we made the trip safely. All of this was nothing new to Philip and me. We had taken so many risks that could have injured or killed us in the past. I hugged Philip and told him I loved him when we left to fly back to Oklahoma.

About two years ago, Patty, my cousin, called me after Sissy's death. I had not heard anything from Philip since that fateful summer. He apparently worked on an oil rig for quite some time, where he smoked and drank every night. He was a heavy smoker. He would smoke one and a half to two packs of cigarettes per day.

I got his phone number and immediately called him. He was living in Texas with his wife, Betty. He had one son, Sam. We probably talked for two hours. We hashed out several things we had done. It was surprising how accurately we remembered things. We talked about his health. I think he had pretty bad COPD, and he stated that the doctors were following a spot on his lung. He was being treated at a VA hospital since he had gone to Vietnam.

Prior to our conversation, I did not know this. I encouraged Philip to seek another opinion. We did not talk about cancer at all. Philip's mother was a heavy smoker, and I think that she died from lung cancer and/or COPD. I would call him two to three times per week on my way home from work. I desperately wanted to go down and see him, but there was just no time. Philip died, probably of lung cancer, about a year later. I just couldn't stop thinking about him and all of the fun that we had together. I did not go to the funeral. I hate funerals. Patty, his sister, did not go to the funeral either. She still lives in California. I guess I wanted to remember him as that very handsome 6'1" sandy-haired guy that stuttered a lot. One of the most incredible things about our phone conversations was that he did not stutter anymore. I really wish that I had seen him. I did speak to his wife. She seemed to be a very caring individual. She probably did not know all of the stuff that Philip and I did in the past.

CHAPTER 27
James Morrison

We were heading to James' house as we had done so many times before. The morning was filled with baseball and football as we had done so many times before. James stopped in the middle of the field and began crying. I asked him what the problem was. He said that they had to move and would probably be put in an orphanage called Oaks. We both sat in the middle of the field and cried for quite some time. I was about ten years old. James was a talented athlete, as I was also. There was another boy who did everything that James did, but he was not a talented athlete like James was; Tommy was his name. I am pretty sure that Tommy was a cousin of James's. The two boys played sports— baseball, basketball, and football. Both excelled in their sports. I think that our best sport was basketball outside of school.

About a week later, I walked across that field one last time. James's house was locked. I looked inside and it was empty. I looked around one last time. James and Tommy were probably put into the Oaks orphanage. His mother was the parent that James and Tommy were living with. I am sure that both of these boys felt betrayed and unloved. They had been sent to the orphanage because their parents could not generally take care of them.

On the way back to my house, I stopped in the middle of the field and again began to cry. Not too long before this, another two friends were sent to another orphanage. For some reason, my mom told me about Vinita, where bad boys and girls are sent. When I got home, I had three friends that were sent to orphanages. I asked her if I would be sent there. She said, "No." I went out the back door and started playing with my toys.

Most of the smaller schools around Salina had basketball tournaments. The most competitive were Oaks, Salina, and Kenwood. Kenwood was a small school that was made up of mainly Cherokee Native American people. They came in year after year from Kenwood, the smaller school that fed into our school. From the stats filled out at the school by the coach, most kids did not go on to high school. The kids' stats were not checked when they were checked in; therefore, Kenwood won most of the tournaments because the kids did not have to send in a birth certificate. Many times they cheated on the weight of their players.

Kenwood had two players that were two years older than the players on our team. This was not checked by the officials at the tournament. It is safe to say that most of the Kenwood players were two years older than other players on other teams. This gave them a distinct advantage. The best two tournaments were Oaks and Salina invitational tournaments. There were three games with a championship game on a Saturday night. For the championship games on Saturday night, there was standing-room only. People were turned away because there was no more seating. Needless to say, there was some fudging going on with the tournaments, especially from Kenwood.

For some reason, age, weight, and grade stats were checked for all of the Salina players at the Oaks tournament. Dwayne Sasser was a key player for our team. We asked the officials if we could have Dwayne exercise to hopefully decrease his weight to below one hundred pounds. They said yes. We put coats on him to work up a sweat and burn calories. We went back for a weight check, and he was down one pound. We had him run around the track several times, and after another weight check, he was down another pound. After exercising more, another weight check revealed his weight to be ninety-nine pounds. We had to play three games, then the championship game on Saturday night. We had a very good team. The three teams were fairly competitive. We beat Kenwood to advance to the championship game against Oaks. This was the first time I had seen James and Tommy since James and I fell to our knees crying in the middle of that field. James and I made eye contact and stared at each other for quite some time. We walked toward each other and hugged each other for the longest time; then the competitive nature in both of us took over.

We had a very good team with Dwayne, James Chuckalock, and me. The gym at Oaks was packed. We were tied at halftime. It did seem like James Morrison and Tommy Powell had adjusted very well at Oaks. The second half of the game was evenly matched, it seemed the shots were traded one after the other. No one was ever ahead by more than four points. We called a time out with thirty seconds to go. Dwayne was to pass the ball to James Chuckalock, and then James passed the ball to me at the baseline. I could see James Morrison coming toward me. I quickly shot the ball from the baseline, and there was nothing but net. We won by two points! Somewhere in the deafening sound of the Oaks' fans was, "Good game." We won the championship game in Salina from my baseline shot by two points. After the game, we hugged each other and talked about our days growing up in Salina. We both said those were precious times in our lives that we will never forget. I honor James's fortitude for overcoming a major adversity in his life, which was admittedly being sent to Oaks as a young boy. I'm sure he was a teacher the students at Oaks could look up to and admire.

I replied, "Good game, James." Little did we know that all of our games in the future were going to be like this. My sources tell me that James enrolled at Northeastern State and became a teacher. He eventually became a principal at Oaks also. My sources tell me that he died of a myocardial infarction, a heart attack, several years ago. We were the same age.

The tournament at Salina was about the same as the Oaks tournament. There were several talented teams. The final four were Kenwood, Oaks, Salina, and Colcord.

In the championship game, it was Salina versus Oaks. I loved shooting from the baseline at our gym. Again, the ball was passed to me. Little did I know that those two boys who sat down in that field crying would come to this point in our lives.

CHAPTER 28
Gary Salyers, My Cousin

Gary was about two years older than me. He was about six foot and about my build. Academically, he was a C minus to occasional B student. An A would have been out of the reach of Gary. He had one brother and one sister. They enrolled in Pryor High School. None of them played a sport. I am sure that both Gloria and Roy had no interest in playing a sport in high school. I really do not know how far Roy and Gloria made it in their academics. I would imagine that it was not all that far.

Gary tried and went out for football. He did not make the team. Gloria wanted Gary to go to Salina public schools because of me. She felt that I would tell him where to go every day. Furthermore, I was unable to locate some of my classes. I was at a different campus the year before. All of this was new to me also. Every day after school, Gary would meet his parents at our house. Gloria wanted me and Gary to tell her how the day went. Gary liked to fight. He obviously was no good at football. We were at the fair in Pryor, Oklahoma, looking at the animals. Gary would go up and ask guys if they wanted to fight. This is how stupid he was. There was a police officer that heard Gary ask a boy if he wanted to fight. The policeman grabbed Gary and told him that he would be thrown out of Pryor fair if Gary asked a boy again. There would also be a fine. The amount, I was uncertain. He did not ask anybody else if they wanted to fight.

Roy and Gloria, when they moved back to Oklahoma, lived on a three-hundred plus acre farm. They were to take care of things on the farm in exchange for living there. There was a young man, cognitively challenged, that could hardly take care of himself. His name was Jimmy Salyers, kinfolk of Roy Salyers. If Gary was my cousin, I must be kin to Jimmy. Gary's father and Jimmy were kin to each other. Gary and Jimmy were cousins. Unfortunately, Jimmy was the butt of terrible jokes, especially at school. Neither Gary, his brother, or his sister played any sports.

Jimmy would roam around town talking to anyone that would listen. He knew when there was recess because he would go to the front of the school where the majority of teachers would go for a smoke. They would make fun of him quite extensively. Jimmy could not discern what they were talking about. Jimmy should have been in a long-term care facility. I feel he would make it much better than where he lives now. Roy, his cousin, should look into this. However, Roy does not want anything to do with Jimmy whatsoever.

Roy and Gloria talked Lillie Mae into putting in an indoor toilet. She had just taken the money from the Grand River Dam Authority (GRDA). Lillie Mae got her money from the Grand River Dam Authority for the farm. I think Roy and Gloria knew this was some easy money. I really do not think the toilet worked all that well anyway. I think the toilet had a major malformation and only lasted two or three years. Grandma wanted the farm to be passed on fifty-fifty. Roy and Gloria told Lillie Mae that she should have all of the farm instead of fifty-fifty. Roy and Gloria took Lillie Mae over to Pryor and got her hooked up with a high-profile attorney. This necessitated Mom to also get an attorney. Mom and Lillie Mae had about three contentious meetings.

Roy and Gloria took Lillie Mae to wherever she wanted or needed to go. Eventually, this was settled without going to trial. Lillie Mae was able to understand what Roy and Gloria were doing to her. She begged Mom to forgive her for what she had done to Mom. From then on, Lillie Mae would not allow Roy or Gloria into her house. Same with Mom. She did not want or let them in the house. Even if they were on the porch, Mom would close the door in their faces. I really do not think that Mom ever recovered from this. She locked both Roy and Gloria out of her house and out of her daily life. Mom just could not get over what they did to her. Although Lillie Mae also locked Roy and Gloria out of her life, I felt that there was something in the back of Mom's mind that would not allow Lillie Mae, her sister, to get as close to Mom as compared with their relationship before. In addition, Roy and Gloria came to see Dad after he was diagnosed with cancer. Gloria was a half sister to Daddy. She came over one time and started telling Dad about the cancer along with after other aspects of Daddy's cancer. There were several disturbing aspects regarding his cancer. When they left, Gloria had put Dad in a state of depression acutely. Dad told Mom to never let Gloria in the house again. Mom did not allow Gloria in the house ever again. I was about ten years old when all of this happened.

Gary asked me and Lige to go with him to look at archeological findings on the river. This was a class from the University of Oklahoma. Lige said that he would not be available to go. I said that I would go with Gary. Lige did not tell me not to go with Gary. We both went to the campsite and had a good conversation with some of the archaeology students. We left after about fifteen minutes. Little did I know that Gary had lit a stick of wood from one of the campsites. He started putting the tents on fire. He was able to light approximately four tents before they saw what was happening. We started running down the road as fast as we could. We could hear motors starting, suggesting that they were coming after us. And I am sure that they were.

We climbed a fence and hid in a huge tunnel. We could hear some people talking, but they were not police or other authorities. After about thirty minutes, there were no lights and no people talking, that we could tell. As mentioned above, Gary knew exactly where he was, whereas I had no idea. He, I am sure, thought losing me was laughable. It was actually dangerous for him to do this. We had swum and walked across Grand River to get to this place. There was no Gary around. I decided to swim back across. I was so tired from swimming across the river. When I reached the other side, I was exhausted. I lay on the bank for probably twenty minutes. I did not have any idea where I was and where to go. I started walking, and soon I heard a horse making a snorting sound. I jumped on the horse by standing on a rock. This horse belonged to Gary and Richard. The horse actually took me to the farmhouse, which was where I needed to go. I found my bed on the floor and fell asleep immediately.

Every Thanksgiving we spent at Gloria and Roy's house. And every Christmas was at our house on December 24. I would never go anywhere with Gary again. I think he is an individual that is hard to trust. Gary was never disciplined by his parents. He was left to his own discretion.

I think Gary, most of the time, could not tell what was good or bad behavior. I think Gloria, his mother, thought that if Gary hooked up with me, his grades would improve. I could not tell Gloria how Gary's day went. This had to come from Gary. I had sports every day after school. As we know, Gary tried to go out for football but could not make the team. In football, he must have been very bad. Gary was not an athlete. Many times, kids like him made the team only for the first team to use for hitting at practice and nothing more. I think he needed to sit at a table where he could be observed until his schoolwork was done. Somebody should have gone over the schoolwork, and certainly, if he did not understand something, they should help him as much as they could. If his grades did not improve, he should have been tested, especially for reading. This is exactly what Dad and Mom did to Sissy and me. We started at 7:00 p.m. and would study until 9:00 or 9:30. He should have also stayed in at recess.

Steve Young (fictitious name) tried to haze me as much as he possibly could. The hazing was regarding Jimmy Salyers. If Gary and Jimmy had the same last name and were kin, and I was kin to Gary, I must be kin to Jimmy. This is how stupid they were. It did not matter; it was something to haze me about, and they did. He had a bunch of cronies who would also try to haze me. It got so bad that I went to the superintendent and principal about this. How were they going to stop or make somebody else, since they were the main instigators of this? I told them if this continued, somebody was going to get hurt. All of this fell on deaf ears. I had to do something because it was getting very bad. I told Steve that I would meet him at a specified time and place. This was near the back of the shop building. I had two long limbs from the bodark tree. I had my long butcher knife. I had four big rocks about the size of a baseball but heavier. I also had brass knuckles for each hand. Steve and his cronies were on time. All of this was out of sight. He did not see any brass knuckles, but he felt them. He came at me with a big right swing; he missed. I came up with a right swing and severely injured his jaw. He fell to the ground, yelling in pain. His buddies were standing ten feet away. I grabbed my large knife and told them not to get any closer. I jumped on Steve, hitting him with the brass knuckles. I got up and started kicking him, hoping to maybe break some ribs. I then told the fucking cowards to take him away. Hazing from any of them would be met with the same treatment. They dragged him to the car. I beat them to the car with the big knife and punched his tires. I then threw the rock through the window, rendering his car useless.

Steve was taken to the emergency room in Pryor. When Steve came back to school about seven days later, in the study hall, he made some kind of remark. I tackled him and started hitting him in the head with one of my brass knuckles. He started bleeding profusely from his mouth and nose. Everybody was panicking. The superintendent and principal came out of their office; by this time, blood was everywhere. I said, "Did I not tell you idiots that somebody was going to get hurt? You are not going to do anything to me. You two are responsible for this. You should have stopped this before it went so far."

After this incident, the principal and superintendent declared that any jokes regarding Jimmy Salyers would be met with punishment. Jimmy Salyers was admitted to a long-term care facility in another town.

CHAPTER 29

Mike Haley

For six years, Mike and I were the best of friends. When I met him that July, little did I know that we would become the best of friends as we did. We both played basketball, baseball, and football. Mike told me that they may be moving back to Oklahoma. I told him that would be great! We could use another good player for the above sports. Indeed, they did move back to Oklahoma, and Mike was with me in the seventh grade. Mike was 6'1" and had a good build. He had an excellent personality, and everybody liked Mike.

The other summer job that we had was a total of four to five weeks during the summertime. Mike and I hauled hay. Mike and I also hauled this to the lofts. The hay had to be put in the loft. The loft was hotter than the outside temperature. If one could stand to be in the loft, you would be cool once the hay was put in the loft. This was a good feeling.

Mike and I would work together hauling hay. Also, for three to four weeks we would work with about four brick layers. Everyone had numerous curse words. Talk about women was extensive. Our job was to carefully carry hot tar to the brick layers. This was an extremely hot job. We usually worked twelve-hour days, including Saturdays. The pay was excellent, but the work was backbreaking. Hooking up with other people was very curtailed. When one got through hauling hay or hauling the tar, one was extremely tired. We were taken to work and home again in the bed of a truck. My dogs loved the cookies that I bought them. They also loved the collars I bought. When we were working these twelve-hour shifts, we seldom hooked up with anyone. We were up at 4:00 a.m. Mom usually fixed a big breakfast.

There was a run-down log cabin with an unkempt yard. Three of the guys passed by the house on their way to school every day. We never saw anyone in the yard or house. We all decided to break into the log house. We went to the yard at the back of the house. It had a six-foot fence all the way around its yard; this was a chain-linked fence. We all climbed the fence, but it was difficult to do. There was a back door with a porch. I was elected to go first. Much to my surprise, the back door was unlocked. We were walking very slowly; immediately to the left was a stairway, and to the right was a living room. I went to my right, and I looked into the big room; I did not see anyone in there. I decided to go up the stairway. Nobody had a flashlight. It appeared that nobody was up in the upper bedroom because there were spiderwebs extensively up there. I did not want to get a spider bite. They can be as bad as a venomous snakebite. There were three guys upstairs and two downstairs. I did see what appeared to be nice ties.

All of a sudden we heard a yell coming from the bigger room downstairs. We all headed for the door downstairs. There was a sound downstairs that sounded like a gun going off. It also sounded like the guy had a problem cocking this gun. Did anybody lose anything? Nobody lost, and we headed to the back door in the log house. There was nobody that came to the backyard. Both Mike and I suffered a puncture wound on both hands. This hurt like hell. We were all lucky that nothing more happened.

There was a black marker on the water tank that showed how much water we had left throughout the summertime. One summer there was hardly any rain whatsoever. The marker showed no water whatsoever. There was no watering the gardens. We had to go and get water from a truck on Main Street. During summertime, we, Mike and I, hooked up with other friends and did something. This particular afternoon, we wanted to climb the water tower and kiss the ball. This particular day, we did not hook up with anybody, it was just us. Why we wanted to do this, I do not know. There was a platform that encircled the water tower. To get to the platform, there was a ladder from the ground to the platform. We could walk around the tank and enjoy the fantastic view. We decided to flip a coin to decide who would go first.

I won the toss. I slowly started climbing. It seemed like the tank was getting bigger and bigger. I was about three-fourths on the way up when I noted the ladder came loose from the tank. The anxiety prevented me from doing anything. The ladder from the ground to the platform was safe and in good condition. I finally was able to put the ladder from the platform to the ball back where it should be. Oh, how I wanted to be the only one to have kissed that ball. It looked as if, if one fell from the ladder, a person would not fall to the platform. Indeed, you would fall to the ground to your death. After gaining my composure, I decided to slowly begin climbing again. I eventually kissed the damn ball and was safely on my way down to the platform. I told Mike that I would suggest he not go up. It was not worth it. Mike and I finally made it back to the ground feeling very lucky. We needed to go by his house, which was about a block and a half away from the water tower. When we were almost on the porch, Mr. Haley took Mike to the backyard, and really, it made clear to Mike that he would not do anything like that again. He was to be at home for the next three days. Mr. and Mrs. Haley were on their porch observing us walking on the platform and me climbing the ladder to the ball.

There was a big field next to Mike's house. The lady that lived there did not have a problem with us playing there. I met with all the guys and told them the problem; basically, he had to be here for three days. After this, everybody came and played flag football. There were about twelve girls and boys that came daily to play. I think Mike and his mother/dad were surprised that everybody came the next day also. This was the place to play for the next two weeks. I did go and ask the lady living there if it was okay for us to go and play football on her property. She was okay with us playing there. I told her there would not be any trash left behind. After two weeks of playing there, we moved on. I did go back and thank her for what she did, allowing us to play there.

I met Mike at the carnival one Fourth of July. This was after Betty and her cousin, and Philip just got through riding the Ferris wheel. Both Betty's and Mike's families were staying at Grandma Haley's house. I told Betty and Mike we would drop by the next day.

Philip and I were going hunting. Grandma Haley's house was on the way to trails down to the river. Mike told me that they were considering moving back to Oklahoma. Betty said her family was not going back to Oklahoma. Mike and his family did move back to Oklahoma shortly before we enrolled in the seventh grade. Mike's and Betty's families would come back two to three times a year, usually. They lived in Brownsville, Texas. Mike was a good athlete.

During the summer months after school, we got together with two to three other guys to do something, especially when Philip was in town for a couple of weeks. Everybody loved Philip; his personality was infectious. He did not participate in alcohol or smoking either marijuana or cigarettes. I think Philip did smoke some. Philip did stutter. Kidding him about this did not bother Philip. I never saw Philip mad.

As a junior in high school, Mike decided he wanted to go with Denise, who was a year younger than Mike. She agreed and Mike was jubilant. He said he loved her enough to marry her. I told him he was moving way too fast. I told him that prior to getting engaged, he needed to talk to his parents, Denise's parents, to let them know what the situation was. "You are way too young to consider this. See, you are in a situation where you have to ask Denise if you can go with Philip and me to walk around town." Furthermore, Denise was one year younger than Mike.

Mike was a good athlete. He played third base in baseball, linebacker in football, and guard in basketball. Betty, his cousin, continued to come back two to four times a year; each time, I saw her.

On our junior year in football, we decided to begin early drills and running. We decided to run to the bridge, which was about five miles away from my house. It was hot and humid. We could take a swim when we got to the bridge. Almost everybody went to the boat landing after football practice. Also, it was a place to take a bath. I hid my soap.

We were getting ready for the regionals in football. Mike was playing halfback. The goal line was five yards away. Mike told me he was going to run over me. I was playing linebacker. Furthermore, I wore three-pound leg weights on each leg. Mike was given the ball. We were both running toward each other. We both hit each other as hard as we could. Mike lay on the ground in severe pain. This is the same way I broke another guy's clavicle. It was so difficult for me to accept what I did to my best friend. We were getting ready for the regionals and we needed Mike desperately. It was suggested that Mike not play football again. He was taken to a Pryor hospital for evaluation. X-rays showed he had a fracture of his clavicle. Mike was given a sling to stabilize the shoulder. He was found to have testicular cancer with metastatic disease. Radiation was started immediately. There was a good chance that this would be cured with radiation.

Mike and Denise finally got married. They had two girls. After Mike and I jumped over the threshold, the double doors entrance to the school, Mike enrolled at Northeastern College. He wrote me, stating he was dating three or four different girls. I was shocked. This was exactly why I was against him getting married. I let my feelings be known again. I think their parents were raising the girls. I think Mike went to Northeastern for two years. I don't know what he was majoring in. He then started having a lot more pain, most likely due to the metastatic disease. He had to drop out of college because of this. He had to move back home with Denise. He had lost a lot of weight. Denise took care of him as best as she could. This was before hospice came upon the scene in medicine.

The summer between our freshman and sophomore year, Mike wanted to go to Tulsa to some bars. Mike was drinking shots of hard liquor, whereas I had one beer. Mike was no way ready to drive home.

I drove to Mike's house and helped him into the house. I told him I would see him tomorrow.

As mentioned before, Mike enrolled at Northeastern. I do not think that Mike had made up his mind about his major or what he wanted to do after graduation. Northeastern was a college in Oklahoma where the majority of teachers go to get their teaching degrees. This is where Dad wanted me to go as well as my counselor. My counselor also wanted me to change my degree from premed to another major, such as teaching. My counselor informed me that nobody from Salina High School had ever graduated from Oklahoma State University (OSU) or University of Oklahoma (OU).

After three weeks of dating, Mike asked Denise to marry him. I told Mike that Mike and Denise needed to speak to their parents regarding their wedding plans. To my knowledge, they had not sat down with their parents to discuss marriage with them. I told Mike that he was moving way too fast. I also told him that they needed to discuss their wedding plans with both sets of parents. I told Mike that they were going to be away from each other quite frequently for long periods of time. I furthermore told Mike, "Going to class is just one aspect of it." There were going to be days that he was going to get caught up studying. Almost every weekend will be filled with study hall. "Where is Denise going to college?" I asked him. I presumed Northeastern, if she was going to go. "There is also a question about who would pay for the expenses. I presume your parents and Denise's parents, if she decides to go to college. This is going to be a big burden for both set of parents. That is, metastatic testicular cancer, was not what they asked for." After football practice, almost everybody went to the boat landing to cool off or to take a bath. I hid my bar of soap so that I did not have to carry it around with me.

On my way back to Oklahoma from North Carolina, I called him, but he did not want to talk. I talked to Denise. She was not doing very well either. Again, her parents were taking care of the kids. Mike died around age twenty-five. Everybody took this very hard. I was able to come back to Oklahoma for the funeral, and I am glad I did. I was able to give Denise a big hug. I told her if she wanted to talk to me about anything; I gave her my phone number. I was going back to Oklahoma for two to three weeks.

The girls were doing okay. Denise's parents as well as Mike's parents were not doing good. Mike's parents were taking this hard, especially since this was their only child. Years later, Denise had remarried. She had two children with this marriage too. It was really good to see her. We talked about old times. Some were good and laughable, and others were so painful. We both agreed that we will never close that chapter in our lives. Mike was buried in the same cemetery where we had hidden behind the headstones and were waving the white sheets; how ironic is this.

Betty also came to the funeral. It was so good to see her. Both of us were stable but having a hard time with Mike's death. We went on a long walk. We had a lot of things we needed to talk about. I told her I was in premed at OSU and was making excellent grades, but it was very hard. All of my waking time, I was reading or studying or going to class. My freshman year, I went out for basketball. Unfortunately, with my knee injured and surgery being needed, I was not doing great because of the continued pain. Betty wanted to know why I did not write more often. I promised her that I would start being more diligent in writing her. I told her that my coursework was very difficult as well as laboratories and chemistry. I said to Betty, "Mike would always tell me how you were doing."

CHAPTER 30
Why I Don't Hunt

My father was a good hunter. Dad was a really good shot. He did not kill just for fun except for snakes. He would let me kill water moccasins, rattle snakes, copperheads with the single-shot shotgun. This gun had such a kick that I could not shoot it a lot; it resulted in the bruising of my shoulder.

Dad would go hunting by himself and come back with three to four squirrels. Dad and I would eat the legs as prepared by Mom. Mom and Sissy would not eat the squirrels. One Saturday, Dad and I were sitting on the small step at the entrance to the kitchen near the back door. We were also near the bodark tree from which I made bows and arrows. The limbs from the bodark tree are how I created my bows. This is the same tree where Dad got the limbs to discipline me. We were looking at all the birds in the tree. All of a sudden, my dad uttered, "Would you like to go and get a BB gun?"

I was stunned, but I told him, "Yes." There was a hardware store on Main Street that had just recently opened. Interestingly, the lady who owned the store was Ms. Allen, the fourth-grade teacher whom I called a witch. I thought I was ready to go bear hunting with this gun. My target was a fifty-five-gallon can. Sissy wanted to know what she was going to get since I got something.

We occasionally went hunting on a Sunday morning. One Sunday in October, when I was ten years old, Dad and I went duck hunting. Mom and Sissy went to Sunday school and church. Dad saw two ducks and pointed them out to me. I hurriedly got my single-shot shotgun in position and pulled the trigger. I hit the female duck. Down came the duck, and when it hit the ground, it was dead. Dad said, "Let's walk away and see what the mallard does." He said, "Maybe you can get that one also." The mallard circled and circled. As we kept walking, the mallard landed near the female duck. He stayed there for the longest time, as if we had killed his mate. Eventually, the mallard flew again, circling as if to say goodbye. Dad said, "Go and get the duck." I walked slowly to the female duck, picking it up. I wondered if the female duck had any ducklings, which might die without their mom.

We took the duck home for Mom to fix for Sunday night dinner. I had not eaten wild duck before. It did smell good. I took one bite and could not eat any more. Dad asked me, "What's wrong?" I responded that it did not taste good. Mom and Dad sure liked it. You can't tell me that when we killed animals, birds, and so on, we kill moms and dads, which has a profound influence on the opposite sex. The circling and landing of the male duck had such a profound influence on me that I never killed another animal or bird. I know me killing the female duck had a profound reaction on the mallard. I wondered what the mallard did, especially if they had ducklings. When I went hunting with Dad or Mr. Piguet, I would shoot either below or above the bird or birds. I therefore never killed again. To this day, those two ducks had such a profound influence on me that I will never shoot another animal or bird to kill it. I never told Mom or Dad what effect this incident had on me. Snakes, fish, I could kill without a problem. But for almost anything else, I would either shoot above or below. I did not want to let Dad feel that I was not enjoying our hunting or walking in the woods. Because of this, I asked the gentleman, when Monroe died, if the gentleman knew if the two mules were sold separately or together. As he said, he thought that they were sold together. To me, that was a lot more tolerable than selling them separately.

Hope rescued two beautiful black Percheron horses. They were mother and daughter about one year apart. One had severe arthritis necessitating euthanasia. Within a day, the other was having such severe abdominal pain more than likely because she was missing her daughter. Before too long, we had to put her down also. I think the mother profoundly missed her daughter.

There were two quarter horses at South Dakota State. When she was going to South Dakota State for school, Hope had a job taking care of the horses in the horse barn. She found out that the school was going to get rid of the two horses. The school did not have any use for them. They furthermore did not have much shelter during the wintertime. They had lived their entire lives together. They did not tolerate being away from each other very well.

When Hope found out the school was going to sell them, she knew one without the other would not be tolerated very well. One was twenty-five years of age, and the other was twenty-six years of age. We bought them and brought them to live together at our farm. They lived out their lives together on the farm for twenty years. They had very good shelter also. One was forty-five, and the other was forty-six. One was blind but was able to keep up with other by smell and touch. One developed arthritis so badly it could not walk; he had to be put down. We knew one without the other would not be tolerated. Both had to be put down together. Both lived an incredible life together.

Do elephants not have family systems? Do wolves not have family systems? Absolutely, they do. If these do, why can't other species also have a family system? I do not blame anyone for hunting. Indeed, hunters can provide a hundred reasons why hunting and killing of birds and animals is good and needs to be done. I challenge the hunter who is so jubilant and wants to have his picture taken because he killed an incredible deer to look into the eyes of that deer and think what you did to that family system.

CHAPTER 31

Hematuria and the Hooker

Mike Haley and I decided we would begin running a week before football practice began to get a jump on the other guys. On our first day, we decided to run to a bridge; it was about six miles out of town. We were juniors in high school at this time. I was one of the halfbacks, and Mike was an end. I also played safety for defense. We were supposed to have a good team; we were picked to be number one in the conference.

On the day of our run, it was a very hot day. We started out from my house; we had played catch with the football beforehand. We were both wearing Converse All Stars shoes on. As one knows, there is very little support with these shoes. Furthermore, we ran most of the way slapping our feet on the hot pavement. Finally, we got to the bridge.

Mike was going to dive into the water; however, I hollered to him that the water was shallow in that area and that he should not dive. We climbed the huge rocks into the cool water; it felt so good. We swam for about an hour, and then we started back home, running all of the way. Again, we were slapping our feet on the hot pavement.

That night, Mike noted blood in his urine. He was alarmed but did not know what to do. Obviously, with our first day of working out, we were sore. The next day, after Sunday school, I told Mike that I had blood in my urine. He turned to me with a bewildered look on his face and stated, "So do I." We went for a short walk discussing what we thought we should do. We did not want to tell our parents yet. We therefore decided to tell our football coach, Hack. Hack was a short, fat man who was a lineman for Pryor High School. Pryor was known to have a good football program. Hack suffered a fracture of his elbow and had to have surgery. Postoperatively, he developed an infection of his elbow and was diagnosed with osteomyelitis. He still had purulent drainage.

After football practice, we told Hack we wanted to talk with him. This was fine per Hack. As we started walking, I told Hack that Mike and I had blood in our urine. After quickly spitting out his big chew of Red Man tobacco, he turned quickly to us and told us, with a big Southern drawl, "You boys got the clap. Do you know how you get that?" We knew that much, but not much more. "You boys' dicks swollen?" Hack wanted to know. We responded no. Hack stated, "You boys' dicks red?" We both said yes. "How did you get the money for this, and what is her name?" I told Coach we had not been with a hooker. We left without any recommendations from the coach.

The next day was Sunday; Mike and I discussed what to do. We did not have any more hematuria. We thought it best to tell our parents. I told Mom and Dad at the Sunday lunch after church. I told them that Mike had it also. Their faces were stunned, and they stared at me for quite some time. I had an idea what they were thinking. They asked me if I was feeling good. I told them yes. That's all that was said for that day.

Mike and I went to the football field that afternoon and ran and threw the football. The next day, Mike and I started in the junior year. In the first hour, we were asked to come to the superintendent's office. We entered together, and we were shocked to see the superintendent, principal, some teachers, and all the football coaches. There were two chairs for us. Mr. Jones, the superintendent, spoke first. He said, "I understand you guys got the clap. We need to know the hooker's name and how much you gave her."

I replied, "There was no hooker, and we have no money to do that with anyway."

Mr. Pierce, the principal, asked, "How you boys' dicks today?" We both answered, "A little red, a little sore." This was probably from the jock support that we had to wear. By noontime, it was all over school that Mike and I had the clap and that we got it from a hooker and that people should stay away from us. The football boys all wanted to know who she was, was she good looking, and so on. Initially, we replied, "You ought to try it," with a laugh. "Want the phone number?" We got as much out of it as we could. We had three other meetings with the same people above. The main thing we wanted to know was how our dicks were. From this time on, they suggested we go to the doctor.

There were no other symptoms, no more urinating blood. We knew that we did not have the clap. By Thursday, we were getting ready for the Friday night football game. I am sure that some of the moms and dads were wondering about this also. I had a run for a touchdown, Mike played an excellent game, and it was basically dropped. Mom and Dad asked me how I was one other time, and I replied, "Normal." Nothing more was said about it.

For years, I wondered why we had the hematuria. In medical school, I learned about march hemoglobinuria, where cadets who are marching slapping their boots on the ground break up the red blood cells, which releases hemoglobin into the bloodstream. The cell that is filtered by the kidney and what is passed out through the kidney is hemoglobin, which gives the urine a red color. There is no harm unless there is a lot of blood in the urine. At the time, there was just something different about Mike. He too noted that his stamina was not the same.

CHAPTER 32

Roger Klinger

Roger Klinger was a short man, around 5'10", who was hired to teach history to the seventh- and eighth-grade classes at Salina. This was his first year of teaching. He had a teaching degree from Northeastern. He also went to Oklahoma State for three years. He loved Oklahoma State University. He went to Colcord High School. He had a friend, Ben, that was from Colcord High School that was a very popular boy at Oklahoma State. He was the president of the student body and was president of the fraternity he was in. His friend, Ben, was into a lot of gambling. This turned out to be devastating for Ben and his family. He had a law degree, which was later taken away because of his gambling.

Roger did not drink or smoke. He taught my sister history and fell in love with her. Roger came to the house a few times and met Mom and Dad. Mom and Dad liked Roger a lot. Before too long, there was an appliance store in Pryor that brought a TV to be set up at our house. Mom and Dad could not believe they were getting a nice TV. It was good for them to sit down after a hard day and watch their favorite TV show. They both fell in love with the TV and Roger. Every Saturday, they loved to watch Hee Haw and Lawrence Welk. Mom really liked to watch Johnny Carson. We still listened to the Grand Ole Opry on Saturday night at nine o'clock. The TV was a very nice gesture by Roger.

Roger as a teacher dating Sissy was against the rules. Mom and Dad were certainly not going to say anything. Nothing was said by the school either. I do not know if the school even knew about Roger and Sissy dating.

Dad was working at McDonnell Douglas in Tulsa. As mentioned, he would get a ride with a gentleman from Spavinaw every morning. Soon, the man from Spavinaw retired, and Dad did not have a way to get to McDonnell Douglas. For a period of time, Dad caught a ride with Mr. Whiteday. His son, Warren, was in my class in school. After Mr. Whiteday retired, Dad had no ride to work at all. If he could get to Locust Grove, he would have a ride to Tulsa; this is where Roger came into play.

Roger and Dad had to leave around 5:30 a.m. in order for Dad to catch his ride in Locust Grove to Tulsa. If Roger was running five to ten minutes late, then Dad would wake me up to run to Roger's to make sure that he did not oversleep. By far, most of the time, Roger was on his way. One day, I asked Dad why he did not drive a car because then he would not have to be dependent on everybody else. He gave no explanation, as usual.

One summer, shortly after school was out, Roger bought forty pigs. They were kept at Lillie Mae's seven-and-a-half-acre farm. It was my job to feed them twice daily, morning and evening. I had to draw water from the well in order to feed them. It was an incredible well. It was a very hard job drawing all the water for the forty pigs. The water from the well was incredibly good and cold. I would have Aunt Lilly pour a bucket of cold water on my head. She would stand on the top step to the kitchen to do it. At that time, we were also cutting wood. After a hard day of cutting wood and feeding the pigs, the water felt so good. After about six weeks, the pigs were sold. Roger got a good price for them.

Roger was probably the one and only individual who was responsible for me going to Oklahoma State University. Roger said that, academically, there was no comparison between Northeastern and Oklahoma State University. Mom was neutral, and Dad wanted me to go to Northeastern. He did not think that I could make it at OSU.

He certainly did not feel that with my major of premed, I would ever get into medical school. He felt that I could not ever be accomplished; I was wasting my time and money. How do you think it felt when I received my acceptance letter to medical school? It was no wonder Mom and I cried our hearts out when she received the acceptance letter.

The road to Locust Grove was horrible, gravel with multiple rocks as big as a softball. Roger had bought a beautiful Thunderbird car. He wanted to minimize the number of trips in this beautiful car to Locust Grove; therefore, he bought a red truck that had seen its better days. It was a stick shift. Roger would use the truck to take Dad in the early morning. I would go feed the pigs, and then we would go chop wood.

Sometimes Roger would go out to the eighty-acre land to start chopping wood. I would meet him after feeding the pigs. Roger needed this job in order to pay for his new Thunderbird. Roger was not a muscular man, and by eleven o'clock, he began to tire. It took him a long time to chop down a tree. The weather was a real killer. It would almost always be in the nineties with high humidity. I would pour cold well water over my head to cool off. This helped me a lot. We would work seven days a week. On the weekend, Dad would go out and spray the stumps with a diesel compound, thinking this would kill the tree. In reality, this was like pissing on the stump. I think this was a hobby for Dad. We were probably spending enough money on Roger's salary and the money spent on the diesel to have a bulldozer to clear off the land, if that was the ultimate goal. Roger made a lot of money selling the pigs. He gave me $200. This helped a lot with my dogs. They loved their new collars as well as the cookies I got them.

One afternoon after feeding the pigs, I was driving home and was stopped at an intersection when a drunk driver hit me on the passenger side of the red truck. There were no seat belts in this old truck. The police came and interviewed both of us. The gentleman who hit me could hardly stand. He was so drunk he could not drive home.

My head had been slammed up against the metal partition separating the front windshield and the passenger window. There was some broken glass, and I had some hand and forearm cuts as well as a major contusion of my shoulder, hand, and forearm. I had a huge bruise and swelling on my forehead and a big black eye on the right side. We never knew what a concussion was back then. I am certain I had one at that time because I had a headache for about a week. The old red truck had dents on the right side, but I was able to drive it home. Shortly after the accident, I was contacted by an attorney several times. Roger did not want me to talk with the attorney. Roger got the money from the insurance company. Nothing more was done for the old red truck.

After about a year of dating Roger, Sissy started dating Don Jones. He was a short, fat boy who thought he knew everything. This did not go over well with Mom and Dad. Don never came to the house. Don was the son of the superintendent of the school. What Sissy saw in Don Jones was unexplainable. Roger continued to come to our house quite a bit.

Roger was still eating breakfast and supper at our house. Sissy's interest in Don Jones began to fade. This was great! Roger, before too long, moved to Adair (where Mr. Winfield was the superintendent). Roger met a lady at Adair High School, and before too long, they were married. Sissy and Roger were cordial to each other. We did not see much of Roger after he was married. Martha, his wife, made sure of that. I could tell Mom missed Roger quite a bit. Roger and Martha would take two to three trips a year; they always drove. I really don't think Roger ever flew in an airplane.

I had a chance to play summer baseball again. Dad did not want me to play summer baseball with a traveling team. The team begged me to play for them. I had no transportation to get to the games. I often wonder what would have happened to me if I had played with this team. Would I have been drafted? Would I have received a scholarship from a major university to play baseball? This we will never know.

The summer in between my junior and senior year, I was going to be an orderly at Baptist Hospital, which was affiliated with Wake Forest Medical School in Winston-Salem, North Carolina. Roger and Martha were traveling to see North Carolina. Roger had never seen the ocean. They took me to Winston-Salem, North Carolina, and dropped me off at Rick Robertson's apartment.

I got a ride with Rick when I could; otherwise, I walked. I found out that Rick died approximately a year ago, 2018–2019. I was very saddened. I do not know why he died.

We lived together that summer and my freshman year of medical school. We had a lot of memories together from those two years. We never got into a major fight. We accepted each other very well, and we got along very well during those two years.

Roger was happy with Martha for about three years. He found out that she was committing adultery. They divorced. Roger was devastated. As before, when they were married, we did not see much of Roger. After the divorce, Roger eventually came back into our family again. Roger was welcomed with open arms. Mom loved him like her son. As before, Roger ate both breakfast and supper at our house. Again, Roger needed an extra job, so he returned to cutting wood with me.

Roger liked teaching at Adair. He taught history to eighth- and ninth-grade classes. He also coached junior high girls' basketball as well as junior high boys' baseball and basketball. Even though Roger and Martha both continued to teach at Adair, they never saw each other. Martha married the man with whom she was having the affair.

The summer when I was finishing at Vanderbilt, it was very hot in Nashville. There was a heat wave that settled over Texas, Oklahoma, and Kansas. The daytime temperature was 110 to 120 degrees. We needed to go to Oklahoma first. Our Toyota Corolla did not have air-conditioning. We had to put ice packs on my kids, Garland and Hope, to cool them off. We put ice on their chest and head. We stayed in Oklahoma for about a week. Mom had a window air-conditioning unit. At night, the temperature was around 110. This heat wave lasted for about one hundred days. Roger had a truck with air-conditioning.

Roger, Mom, Linda, Hope, and Garland rode in the air-conditioned truck. We spent the night at Sissy and Robert's house.

Roger went three years to Oklahoma State University and one year to Northeastern, as previously mentioned. He always wanted to be a teacher. His mother was a teacher at Colcord High School. Roger was an excellent teacher as well as an excellent coach. Roger made it known several times to Mom and Dad that I should go to OSU and not to Northeastern. Mom and Dad liked Roger's advice very much and respected his opinion. If it had not been for Roger, I probably would have been forced to go to Northeastern.

Roger wanted me to go with him to see his dad in a Tulsa hospital. He was diagnosed with polycystic kidney disease, which can be hereditary. He needed a kidney transplant; he did get one after about eight months. Before the transplant, he was on dialysis. There was a very strong resemblance between Roger and his father. Roger felt good health-wise, so he did not see any need to go to his physician and get evaluated for polycystic kidney disease. I am sure at that time that Roger had marked hypertension, which meant further decline in his kidney functions.

Roger liked to dress with good taste. He did have very good taste in clothing. He taught me exquisite dressing techniques. There was a store in Tulsa called Orbacks, an incredible men's clothing store. I have not ever seen another men's store like Orbacks in to Tulsa. Every time Roger went Tulsa, he loved to go to Orbacks and pick out a sports coat or a tie; it would take Roger three to four hours to pick out a tie.

Every year for several years, Mom, Roger, Sissy, and Robert would come for the Fourth of July and again at Christmastime. Our children loved the interaction with them. At Christmastime the children got gifts from our visitors. One Christmas, Mom, Roger, Sissy, and Robert were having a problem. Sissy and Robert felt that Mom was being used by Roger. They believed she did everything for him. Mom had previously told them that this was not an issue. They rode up in separate cars. Mom rode with Roger.

When they arrived at our house, one could tell that there was a problem. They did not sit in the same room. They did not eat in the same room. I did see what Sissy and Robert were seeing; Mom was doing everything for Roger. I decided to talk with both pairs separately. Something had to be done. This was not appropriate behavior.

I went riding with Sissy and Robert first. Their main contention was that Roger wanted Mom to do everything for him. This was not a healthy relationship for Mom. Mom was beginning to show signs of fatigue. Dad had done the same thing with Mom, and now she was in another "relationship" where someone wants her to wait on them hand and foot.

I went riding with Roger next. I asked Roger if he felt there was a change in his relationship with Robert and Sissy. He could not detect this. I told him that Sissy and Robert felt that Mom was waiting on him too much and that Mom was showing signs of fatigue. I didn't know who was at fault; Mom would never tell Roger that she needed to slow down. I told Roger to try to decrease his demands on Mom to do things for him.

Roger took this the wrong way. I don't know why he couldn't see how he was using Mom too much. When he got back to the house, he packed his clothes and left. I tried to talk with him. I wanted to have a family discussion, but Roger would have none of it. I don't know if he did not want a discussion regarding Mom because he knew he was using Mom too much or just what he was thinking. Mom packed her clothes and left with Roger. I know Mom loved Roger, but not to the degree that she would forgo her relationship with her daughter, son, and all her grandchildren.

Mom and Roger left around 9:00 p.m. I hardly saw Roger after this incident. From this time forward, Roger spent Christmas with his brother Larry and his children. I do feel that Roger's not wanting to have a family discussion regarding Mom was inappropriate behavior. This really hurt me. This was one of the worst Christmases I had ever had. Mom continued to come up every Fourth of July and every Christmas.

She would fly to Chicago and have me pick her up at the airport. She would occasionally ride up with Sissy and Robert.

About two years later, Roger noted marked fatigue, shortness of breath, palpitation, chest pain, and swelling of his legs. He went to his family physician, who obtained blood for tests and an abdominal ultrasound. Roger had the same thing as his father, polycystic kidney disease. He was also found to be in kidney failure as well as having cardiomyopathy. He was started on dialysis three times a week. This forced him to retire. Mom waited on him hand and foot. Roger wanted Mom around as much as possible, and so she was. About four months later, Roger had a kidney transplant. Mom again was with him 24/7. Roger really had no one else to care for him.

After Dad died from his melanoma, Roger and Mom went on a vacation two to three times a year. They also went to Branson, Missouri, three to four times a year. They saw more of the United States than I probably ever will. Mom enjoyed these trips immensely. Along the way, Roger bought a red Corvette, his dream car of his lifetime. It was a spur-of-the-moment decision.

Roger developed severe chest pain and shortness of breath. He was taken to a hospital in Joplin, Missouri. He had severe diffuse coronary artery disease. He underwent emergency coronary artery bypass grafting. He was also found to have severe cardiomyopathy.

Roger wanted me to talk with his surgeon, which I did. The surgeon informed me that Roger's heart was severely damaged from coronary artery disease and his severe cardiomyopathy. I did not tell Roger this information. His recovery progress was very slow. I talked to his surgeon about every other day, and I would then inform Roger of his progress. Roger, eventually, was discharged to his home. Mom was with Roger 24/7 almost all the time. Roger never recovered from his surgery. He died of multisystem failure. Mom took this very hard. It was as if one of her children died.

Roger's death was so hard for me to accept also. I knew from talking with his surgeon that death could happen at any time. I was therefore not surprised when he did pass. I owe much gratitude in life to Roger. We were very good friends. Before he died, I did tell him what he meant to me and that I loved him. I remembered all of those days of very hard work cutting wood. Roger's death was therefore very difficult for me to accept.

Mom and Dad loved Roger as if he were a child of theirs. I think he was the deciding factor as to where I was going to college. I think it was a big issue when I did not attend Northeastern.

CHAPTER 33
Oral Roberts Basketball Camp

Oral Roberts was seen a few times watching us play. He was very surprised at how we played. He pulled me from the team after our lunch break. But none of this was done. Auntie Ann and Ed did ask me to stay at their house during the Oral Roberts Basketball Camp; that was really a good time. Uncle Ed took me in the morning, and they were there in the afternoon to pick me up. I got to know Oral Roberts himself. He told me to come to his office when it was convenient for me. I did, and at that time, he wanted me to come to ORU to play baseball and basketball. He said that he had been watching me play for the last four days. I told him I had been accepted to OSU in premed and as a walk-on for their basketball team. He told me he wanted me to think about his offer. He also said that I could go to ORU at no cost to me. I told him I would think about it.

I discussed this with Mom, Dad, and Roger. I prayed about this too. Everyone that I talked with suggested that I go to OSU. If good grades were made, OSU would give me more of a chance to get into medicine in comparison with going to ORU for four to five years. I met with Oral Roberts again. I told him with that after much deliberation, I had chosen OSU. He was very disappointed. He stated that if I changed my mind, all I had to do was give him a call. I thanked him profusely for his offer.

As time went on, Oral Roberts University was growing by leaps and bounds. He built an incredible baseball field. He also developed a huge Evangelical portion of his university. He also built a huge arena not only for basketball but also for other uses. ORU reached the Sweet 16 in March Madness in 2021. The baseball program is frequently in the top 25 baseball ranking. I kept his offer in the back of my mind because if I was making Bs or Cs at OSU, then ORU would be a choice to make.

CHAPTER 34
My Acceptance to Medical School

The summer between my junior and senior year of college at Oklahoma State University, I worked as an orderly at the hospital affiliated with the Wake Forest University School of Medicine. An orderly does whatever the head nurse wants done. I would stand near the nurses' station to make myself readily available. I very much enjoyed my work that summer.

Roger and Martha were heading to the beach. I do not think that Roger had ever seen the ocean. I don't know if his wife had seen the ocean at that time. I needed some transportation to the hospital. Roger, a family friend, and his wife took me to Winston-Salem, North Carolina, that summer for my job as an orderly. I needed some transportation back and forth from the hospital to home. They got a newspaper and found an ad in the paper wanting to sell a bike. They went to get the bike, which was for sale for $10. The next day, I was to be at the hospital at 11 a.m. The area had some steep hills. Little did I know the handlebars on the bike were loose. I had no way of tying the handlebars. I was so damn mad that I pushed the bike behind a house and left it there.

I was staying with a first-year medical student. His name was Rick Robertson. He graduated from the University of North Carolina at Chapel Hill. He was an excellent source of information. I got a ride to the hospital when it was available to me. Rick and I did well together that summer. He told me that if I got accepted, I could stay with him during my first year in medical school. We did get along very well. I was learning a lot as an orderly.

During that summer, I had an interview with Dr. Maynard, who was in charge of medical school acceptance. It was an excellent interview. Dr. Maynard was so nice and a gentleman. I informed him that I was working at the hospital as an orderly. After about a month into my senior year, I got a phone call from Dr. Maynard wanting information from my family physician regarding my peptic ulcer disease.

It is hard to explain how I felt. I did not know I was going to get in, though I had a GPA of 3.8 out of 4.0. The interview process was excellent. I filled out forms before the interview. I had my interview with Dr. Maynard before I went back to OSU because I was working as an orderly at the hospital. He was impressed by this. About two years prior to Dr. Maynard calling Dr. Cameron, I had followed up on the peptic ulcer disease.

Dr. Cameron wrote back to Dr. Maynard that I did not have any sequelae of peptic ulcer disease. He did not feel that I would have a problem in the future. Shortly thereafter, I received a letter from Wake Forest Medical School informing me of my acceptance to Wake Forest Medical School. This letter came to my home. Mom received the letter from Wake Forest Medical Center informing me of my acceptance. I had just finished my morning classes. She wanted to see me. She called the FarmHouse Fraternity; this was the fraternity I joined between my sophomore and junior year at OSU. It was a fraternity made up mainly of premed, prevet, predental, and prelaw students. One had to have a fairly good grade point average to get in and be accepted by this fraternity.

As usual, I walked slowly to FarmHouse Fraternity. I walked through the front door, and as I walked down the stairs, I saw the message that my intern had written in big letters, "Congratulations, you have been accepted to Wake Forest Medical School." I could not believe it. This was immeasurable for both me and Mom. I called Mom and we both started crying. As Mom said, they were happy tears. I asked Mom to read the letter to me three different times. Mom met Dad at the porch and told him that I had been accepted to medical school. Mom said that

Dad gave her a big hug with tears in his eyes. Before this, he felt that it was unlikely that I would be accepted to medical school. Everyone felt this was unlikely except Mom and me. Dad wanted me to go to Northeastern to be a teacher. There is nothing wrong with being a teacher if that's what your aspirations are. My aspiration was to be a physician. Dad thought going to OSU would be an unlikely path to being accepted into medical school. Being a senior, I had all of the hard subjects behind me. Indeed, I had to have a required activity. I picked bowling.

In high school, we had to declare a major. My high school counselor, whose name was Mr. Thompson, wanted to discuss my major with me. I had an excellent grade point average. Mr. Thompson asked me what I wanted to major in. I told him premed or physiology. Mr. Thompson leaned back in his chair and asked, "Don't you think you should pick another subject for you to major in?" I told him no, and if he wanted to, he could put physiology as a major for me. Mr. Thompson again leaned back in his chair and stared at his wall for a very long time and said, "Don't you think we should pick another subject?"

I said, "No, that's what I want to do. I want to become a physician." The pressure was markedly decreased. I told Mom I would like to come home for the weekend. Roger came and got me. With Mom, Dad, Sissy, and Roger, it was like old times. Mom met me on the porch, and we both started crying. Mom said she had prayed for this day for a long time. I told her that I had also. I also told Mom that I had met a girl in North Carolina. Mom wanted to know all about her.

Linda was with another girl standing by an elevator when she caught my eye. I met her again, three or four more times. One of the times I met her was when we were moving a patient from one bed to another. I had dated another nurse who lived in the same building. I would take a blade of grass and put it between my thumbs and blow between my thumbs. We eventually started seeing each other every afternoon. We could not go anywhere because neither one of us had a car. Tommy, Linda's brother, came to get me shortly before I left to return to Oklahoma to finish my senior year at OSU. We kept in touch with letters and phone calls. I did tell her I was dating Miss Oklahoma. She felt that this was the end of us. I did call and tell her that with my acceptance to Wake Forest Medical School, it was more than likely the school that I would attend. I made sure that Mr. Jones, the superintendent, Mr. Pierce, the principal, and my counselor Mr. Thompson knew that I had been accepted to medical school. These three people did everything they could to prevent me from going to Oklahoma State University. Shame on you three.

Chapter 35

Bob Piguet

Bob was a teacher who was hired to teach science and math. It was my senior year. I heard we were going to have a new teacher. For some reason, our class was made up of all boys; four to be exact. I will never forget walking into class and meeting Bob. He was morbidly obese and about 6' tall. He struck me as a very funny individual. After the bell rang, he told the class what he expected from us. He told us that he loved photography and that he has set up a dark room to develop photos. He had a 35mm camera which took excellent photos. There were a lot of photos taken, especially of the sporting events that were played. He was at almost all events. All of these photos were developed in the dark room.

In the beginning he taught us about physics; we were to work the problems we were given. For some of reason he very much enjoyed being around Mike Haley and me. Everybody loved being around him, also. We could joke about his obesity without him being offended. I never saw Bob mad or extremely sad.

Bob loved to hunt. He had a motorboat. From September to the latter part of November, we would go duck hunting on the lake. It was illegal to do hunting like that on a boat. It was also illegal to hunt without a license, which we did. In October to the latter part of November, it was extremely cold. I had a single-shot, which had an incredible kick to it. It would injure my shoulder such that I could not lift my arm.

Bob would drive the boat, and Mike and I would huddle behind him. Bob was morbidly obese and would be hot and sweating while

Mike and I would be cold. He would holler to us, right or left when we were coming up on some geese or ducks, on either the right side or the left side of Bob. That was our signal to look in the appropriate direction where Bob spotted either ducks or geese. With my single shotgun, I had only one shot. By the time that I had my gun reloaded, we were beyond the target.

One Saturday, we were out on the lake hunting, me, Bob, and Mike. We spotted an area where there were a lot of what looked like ducks or geese. We could not tell for sure. As we approached, they began to fly. We shot several of them. We took them to show Mom at the Dotson grocery store, where Mom was working. We had Mom come out from the store and look at what we had. Dotson came out, and he was looking at them and said, "Guys, I don't think they are really geese or ducks." Mom, on Sunday morning, cooked one like she would as if it was a goose or a duck. We came home from church. The house had an atrocious smell coming from the oven. Mom had to empty the oven and throw the inside to the compost pile. On Monday, I told Mike and Bob what happened. Bob said his brother told him that what we shot was a buzzard that was on the endangered species list. Bob said it would have been very costly if we had been caught by the wildlife people. No licensed hunting with a boat and killing a bird on the endangered list all would have been very costly for all of us. Thank goodness we were not caught.

On one occasion, we were seen by the game warden. He was hollering to us, telling us to stop hunting with the boat. We did, in the area close to the bridge. We turned and went north. When the bridge was out of sight, we started shooting again. All he had to do was to go to the boat landing and wait for us. We slowly motored up to the boat landing. We did not see anything or anybody. We went into high gear and got the boat stationed appropriately. We went home as quickly as we could. I came in with the shotgun, telling everybody that we did not kill goose or duck when we were on the boat. For some reason we went fishing about five different times.

We had, as a senior class, three different things that were going on at the same time: the senior class play, Chouteau day and building of the float, and senior class trip.

Bob was so popular that the senior class wanted him and Ms. Jetton to be our counselors of the senior class. I was senior class president. It seems like we had a major meeting every day trying to get things set up for our senior class outing. We had pretty much decided on a road trip to western Oklahoma. We also had Pierre Chouteau day coming up. Auguste Pierre Chouteau (pronounced "Show-tow") was a person that would come up the river and dock near Salina to trade with the local Native American tribes. We needed to get going on a theme and building the float. Everybody had a job to do. We needed two small trees and an evergreen tree.

One Chouteau day, Warren Whiteday and I were responsible for this. We pulled up to this house just outside of Salina to see if we could get what we needed, that being an evergreen tree and two other trees. The old man said, "No." We stopped a little way down the road and started cutting down an evergreen and two smaller trees. Little did we know that the man followed us and caught us sawing down the trees. We were on the roadway and not on his property cutting down these three trees. He was somewhat mad at us. I had $20 on me. I asked him if he would take $20 for the three trees. In the beginning he said no. We told him why we needed these trees and that we were seniors at Salina High School. After a while, he said he would take the $20 for them. We both agreed that we were lucky; it was possible something worse could have happened. We also needed a raccoon for our theme. This we stole from the eleventh grade. We kept him in our cellar house. We were all set. Our float for Chouteau day got first place.

Bob drove a truck. He had a canvas elevated about three feet above the bed of his truck. This was a good place to store the cross and the sheets. We also had the senior class play coming up. We were practicing at night for the senior class play. Every night, after we practiced the play, we went to a graveyard, which was just outside of Salina. We had crosses with sheets that we were waving back and forth. There were three guys who were supposed to bring the girls to the graveyard. They were afraid and started to run to the car. We did this for probably about fifteen minutes and then stopped. The next day, they were of the opinion that I and Mike Haley were instigators in this. We had a cross and a sheet draped over it; we were waving the sheet.

It was seven to ten days before the play was scheduled. We were too busy with waving the sheets in the graveyard rather than learning our lines. Ms. Jetton was very concerned about our inept performance. I saw her crying. As senior class president, I called all of the people who were in the play together and told them what I saw, saying that we needed to work on our play and get our lines down. That is exactly what we did. We had an excellent showing as far as the senior class play was concerned. People at the school and class parents filled the auditorium. With all of this going on, we were out of school for three to four weeks. We got unbelievable adulation for all three. I know we did not think it was going to work out all that well, but it did! And some people were saying our senior class play was the best play they had ever seen.

As time went on, more time was spent in the photo lab and less time doing classwork. I eventually had to tell Bob that we needed to do some classwork. Bob had applied for his master's and PhD work at Oklahoma State. We eventually met Loretta, Bob's wife. We invited her to go on our senior class trip. She was as funny as Bob. She accepted the invitation to go on the senior class trip. He knew that I had been accepted to OSU. In addition, the senior class had decided that we were going to go on a trip to western Oklahoma. It was common to have a class trip. There were about thirty kids on the trip; all of the parents let their kids attend the trip. We spent three days and two nights. It was a good class vacation. There were no incidents of drinking alcohol that I know of. I do not know if the guys got any alcoholic beverages to western Oklahoma was pretty much set. If they were to get caught, more than likely, if alcohol was found, and the person was playing a sport, they would more than likely be penalized and not be able to play some games. The question was, was this fair to other members of the team?. That was really between Bob and the boys. I know that I did not have any. There was an incident where one of the girls stole something from a shop that we were in. She eventually had to buy the stolen item.

Bob introduced me to the 35 mm camera and film. He took photos of Garland Jr. one time when he was at our house. I was so impressed with the quality of the photo that I went out and bought a Nikon camera for me and my family. We still have the photo and the 35mm camera.

I had several conversations with Bob about my dreams. I asked him several questions about college, which he was more than adequately familiar with. He would tell me to work hard and never give up on my dreams. I did not know at that particular time that he was applying to OSU for his master's and doctorate degrees. The conversations were different from the rest of the teachers. My counselor, Mr. Thompson, encouraged me to go into something else. I told him that I planned on going into premed. Even my father told me I should be a teacher. I told Dad that there was nothing wrong with being a teacher but that it was not what I wanted to go into.

I was accepted at Oklahoma State University. I told Bob about this. He congratulated me. He wanted to know what I was going to major in. I told him premedicine.

After I got into college at OSU, it seemed like 50 percent of the new freshmen wanted to major in premedicine. This, obviously, was a very competitive major. Bob did not encourage me to go into anything else. He was encouraged by me wanting to go into medicine. I knew it was going to be tough, but that was fine. I welcomed the challenge. He told me that I was going to have to study hard. He stated that I could certainly do it, but it would take a lot of focus.

Bob, I, and Mike Haley went to Tulsa three to four times to watch the cars racing on a dirt track. Bob's brother had been racing for four to five years. Bob's brother was very good. Bob found a car and started auto racing. Bob did not want to get into an accident. Mike and I were given passes so we could go down to where the cars were to help Bob in any capacity that he wanted. We all had a good time taking care of the cars.

When Bob was accepted to OSU for his degrees and needed help moving his furniture to Stillwater, Mike and I helped him.

For a couple of weeks after school started, I was on crutches. I told Bob where I would be for my last class. He still had that canvas on the bed of his truck that came in very handy. I would throw my crutches onto the canvas.

For some reason Bob, I, and Mike went fishing only about four times. We were after catfish, perch, and bass. We ate everything that we caught. We would clean every one, and Mom would fry the fish. They were certainly good.

To my knowledge, Bob did not go hunting, fishing, or drive his car on the dirt track once school started. Every Friday after class, I would walk to Loretta and Bob's place in Stillwater. Sometimes I would eat; sometimes I would play with the black cat.

My counselor, Mr. Thompson, encouraged me to major in something else. My father also told me to go into teaching at Northeastern. Dad had not discouraged Sissy's college choice. I told Dad that there was nothing wrong with a teaching degree but that it was not what I wanted to do. I told him I had to follow my dreams.

When I was at Vanderbilt for my gastroenterology training, Bob and Loretta came to see me. They wanted to go to the Grand Ole Opry. That's exactly what we did. They loved it. It was so good to see them. I took them around Nashville. They did go to stay at a hotel for sleeping. I do not think that one of my beds would have been able to support them. I remember seeing his bed when we were moving him to Stillwater. The bed was made out of two-by-fours and cement blocks.

Bob and family were going on a vacation. There was Bob and Loretta in the front seat and his two girls in the back seat. They were all morbidly obese. Bob was driving. As they drove across a railroad crossing, their car came to an abrupt stop. The car that they were driving got hung up on the railroad tracks and the frame of the automobile. There was just too much weight in the car. They did have their seat belts on, thank goodness. I think otherwise there would have been some contusions along with bleeding. They were very lucky that there was not more trauma than coming to a sudden stop. They had to forgo their vacation.

For a couple of weeks, I would be at my last class, and Bob would come by and get me with my crutches. I would throw my crutches on the canvas top, and away we went. There was no way that the crutches were going to blow away. If I would have to walk all the way, it would have taken me probably an hour and a half. I also had books that I was carrying. I do not know how I made it, but the good Lord gave me the ability to do this.

I was to have surgery on the other side of my left knee. Dr. Coker did examine my left knee and leg and the diagnosis of DVT (deep venous thrombosis). The pain and difficulty ambulating was even much worse than the last time I saw him. He wanted treatment of DVT, which was a heating pad and moist cloth to the leg and knee, and probably within two weeks, I developed a terrible case of jock itch. We did get some medication over the counter, which did an excellent job resolving this. This came about because of the heating pad and moist clothes. I spent three weeks lying on my back with the heating pad and moist heat to the calf without any improvement whatsoever. In addition, the temperature was midnineties. The heating pad and warm soaks made things worse. The heating pad made things really hot. We did not have air-conditioning.

As mentioned above, nothing was improving; it was perhaps even worse. The DVT did not improve. I saw Dr. Coker again. He examined my knee and calf and said, "We might as well go ahead and operate. You've had three weeks of worsening pain in the knee and calf." In addition, I was to start college at Oklahoma State in one week. I saw Dr. Coker, and he was good with proceeding on to do the surgery.

We proceeded with the surgery, and it was incredible that the DVT resolved. I had no pain in the calf whatsoever.

I was discharged on Sunday, and Roger, I, and Mom went to Stillwater to get me started at OSU. I was to be on crutches for two weeks.

Bob told Loretta that he was going to go lie down, that he felt excessively tired. After about an hour, she went in to awaken him for supper. He was unresponsive. Mom called me and told me about this. At Mom's funeral, I saw Loretta and one of her girls. I sat with them, and we talked about old times for an hour or so. I played so many times with their black cat. Bob was on his way to getting his doctorate degree, which I think he mentioned would take around two years that he would have to be doing this. I wanted Loretta to know that she and Bob filled a very large part in my life when I started at OSU. I told Loretta that I bet Mom and Bob are in heaven dancing, Bob probably playing an instrument, a bass, and Mom singing, which she did quite a bit. She sang in the congregation at church too. Sometimes it was more humming than singing. I miss both of them very much.

CHAPTER 36
Left Knee Injury

It was the first football game of the season. We expected to have a good season. The projection was that we would come in first or second in our conference. I was to have a good season running and passing. We had James Chuckalock, a Cherokee Native American who was 6'6", and usually, he had two to three guys hanging on him and he was still able to run. There was a play in which I was to pass to James Chuckalock, which was accomplished. James usually required two to three boys to bring him down. It was a pass to James from me. My left knee was planted when somebody hit me at the knee level as I was about to throw the ball. My leg seemed weak. After the game was over, my left knee was weak with some pain. With pain and swelling, there was considerable pain throughout the night.

The next day, Saturday morning, around four o'clock, I was to go to the farm and continue cutting wood with an ax and chain saw. I had trouble walking. I could not bend or straighten my knee. We went to see Dr. Cameron, our family physician. He said that he thought I had a bruised knee and that I should apply warm soaks to the knee. He said there should not be any running at all. He did give me some exercises to do, which I accomplished. He did an X-ray, which did not reveal any fracture. He suggested resting as much as possible. I got out of cutting wood for that day. I think Roger and Dad went and worked. As the day progressed, the pain was decreased and the range of motion was better. Dr. Cameron seemed adamant against doing any surgery whatsoever. He did show me some exercises to strengthen my knee. Rest and warm and cool soaks to the knee really helped a lot. These things were helping, but I could not play football or any other sport at this point. The pain in the knee was very severe when I tried to bend or extend my knee. The football team was not having a stellar year. The team was in the middle of the conference. With resting of the knee, the pain did decrease to about a 2 out of 10 on the pain scale. I spent my six to eight weeks rehabbing my left knee.

Again, we were to have a good team in basketball. We had James Chuckalock at 6'6" and me at 6'3" and Mike Haley at 6'0". I did not know the status of Mike's clavicle. He told me things were "good." It seemed he did not have the stamina that he used to have. The first basketball game went well. I did not have any severe knee pain. I was able to play the entire game without a problem. If the season went this way, we would have an incredible team. After the game, I could feel some mild pain, probably 4–5 out of 10. Everybody was talking about how good of a team we were going to have.

Again, I was supposed to cut wood on Saturday morning. I could detect some increased pain as the night went on. The next morning, I was having severe pain with an inability to extend or contract my knee. Roger was at the house around 7:00 a.m. Somebody had told Roger that there was an orthopedic surgeon that I could go and see. He did sports medicine for the University of Arkansas. Roger called the surgeon and for us to meet him at the Fayetteville Hospital ER in Arkansas. We went. The surgeon, Dr. Coker, was a short man with a very pleasant personality. He had some ortho problems of his own.

Saturday morning, it was evident that I could not go and cut wood all day. At seventeen years old, a senior in high school, I was having problems walking on my left leg. I gave the surgeon the history of what happened. He put me through several maneuvers, all of which were very painful. I told him that we had seen another physician who was actually our family physician, who emphatically stated that surgery did not need to be done. Our family physician gave me some exercises to do, along with warm soaks to the knee. That did help, but I still could not extend or flex my knee to a great extent. I skipped the football season since my knee was not back to normal. I started back to sports playing basketball. I told the surgeon we had a game "last night." The pain in my knee markedly increased after the basketball game. The next day, Saturday, the pain was incredible, and again, I could not extend or flex my knee.

Dr. Coker did say that if I rested my knee, perhaps for a month to six weeks, the knee would be better. But just like for the last six months, the knee pain was much better. But he told me that if I went out and tried to do strenuous exercises like basketball and catching, he felt that the pain and decreased range of motion would be present again. The only way to help my knee get back to normal was surgery and exercises for the knee.

Dr. Coker felt that my inability to extend or contract my knee was perhaps a piece of cartilage in the knee joint itself. He was not going to know for sure until the surgery. He stated that he was going to put me in the same room as a boy who was going to have shoulder surgery.

Dr. Coker got me admitted to the hospital on Sunday morning with surgery to be done on Monday morning. The other boy was checked in around 4:00 p.m. We got to know each other very well. His father was with him. He was an All-American quarterback at the school that he was attending. He had an incredible following. He wanted to be in premed at the University of Arkansas. I told him that I was considering going that route myself. He told me that there were going to be a few girls coming by just to say hello. I told him to be thankful for his friends as well as academia that he had at his school as I had neither one of these.

Visitation was at 5:00 p.m. Right at five o'clock, we had about ten girls come in and visit us. Of course, I had to tell everybody my story and that my surgery was the next day. The other boy's surgery was to follow mine. People were sitting on my bed as well as Scott's bed. The girls had numerous questions for me. They asked me where I was going to go to college and what I was majoring in. I told them that I was more than likely going to go to OSU and enroll in premed. They wanted to know if I was going to play any sports at OSU. I told them hopefully basketball. The girls that came by were mainly freshmen from the University of Arkansas. They stayed until nine o'clock. There had to be another twelve to fifteen girls who came by, wishing us well. I was tired and so was Scott. We fell asleep fast. We were both going to have a busy day tomorrow. I awoke early, but I could not have anything to eat. I did have some ice chips. I did not wake up until midafternoon.

I was in a lot of pain. They brought Scott back into the room around the time I awoke. I received intramuscular injections of Demerol and occasionally morphine for the pain. This put me back to sleep. I woke up around five o'clock with a beautiful girl sitting on my bed and staring at me. Came to find out she was Ms. Fayetteville, Arkansas. She was not a part of the original group of girls that had come by on Sunday. I had a very nice conversation with her. She asked me to tell her my story. Everybody wanted to listen, so I told it. She was still in high school with Scott. She knew Scott very well. She wanted to know if I wanted any ice chips. I told her, "Yes, that would be great." I did find out that Scott was an All-American high school quarterback. He wanted to go to Arkansas to play football and to major in premed.

I could see why she was Ms. Fayetteville. Her name was Olivia. I thought that all of this was incredible, that we both got hurt in football, both of us needed surgery, both of us wanted to go into premed, and we were both heavily into other sports, Scott in football and me in basketball.

Again, around five o'clock, all of the girls who came by on Sunday stopped in on Monday to see how we were doing. There had to be twelve to fifteen girls that came by to see how we were doing. They fed Scott and me ice chips along with our food for the day. We really appreciated this. They also brought in other sandwiches for us to eat to supplement the hospital food. We were both very thankful for them doing this.

The next morning, Tuesday, when Dr. Coker was making rounds, he came into the room and bent my knee. I let out a holler because it caused incredible pain. He said he knew I was going to have that response. He wanted to determine how much pain we were in. The physical therapy department was going to give us exercises to do. I could not believe the loss of muscle strength in such a short period of time.

Olivia came back to the hospital around four thirty, before everybody else came. She helped me eat, and boy did that food taste good. She also gave me ice chips again, which tasted very good. She also gave Scott ice chips, which he enjoyed. Scott told me that the senior class in his high school was having a big party, about ten days after our surgeries. Olivia told Scott she would like to go with me to the party. Scott discussed this with me a little later. I asked Olivia if she would go with me. She told me that she would love to go with me. I could not tell, from all the girls that had been coming to see us, who Scott would take. It seemed that every night there were more girls, and different girls were coming by. After everybody cleared, Olivia was the last one to leave. I thanked her for her help. I asked Scott whom he was going to take; he replied Joan. I asked Scott to introduce her to me the next day. I told him I hoped to be out of the crutches before the party. I got Scott's phone number, as well as Olivia's phone number.

We discussed our different surgeries and how our healing was going. I could see how Scott was a very popular boy in his school. Academically, he was great, along with sports; obviously, he was great. Dr. Coker gave me four tickets to the University of Arkansas and OSU basketball game. The seats were right behind the players' seats. It was a good game. OSU won!

The dance was one week away. The pain and range of motion was getting better. I could not attend the dance and also drive back home. Scott said I could spend the night with him, which I did. He had a very nice family. He had one brother and one sister. It is of note that almost all surgeries are performed arthroscopically in the 2000s. This decreases the pain and swelling as compared with the surgery that we had done. I kept in touch with Olivia for quite some time after meeting her. I do think Scott was admitted to med school at the University of Arkansas. Interestingly enough, Dr. Coker had graduated from Wake

Forest Medical School. Furthermore, his son became an orthopedic surgeon in sports medicine at the University of Arkansas.

The basketball team did not win a game until I came back halfway through the season. After about three games, we did develop into a good team. We won two tournaments that we were in. My knee injury did markedly result in muscle atrophy which did affect my jumping and cutting ability. Even though doing exercises to strengthening my left leg, I was never able to get it back to normal. I was still able to score 18–20 points per game. Me quitting sports in college was made for me, i.e., the knee injury. I have often said that my knee injury gave me the ability o become a physician. I do not think I could have had the grades I had at OSU and played basketball at OSU. At OSU, I did not know anyone in Premed that also played a sport. There was just not enough time to do both.

MY EDUCATION IN SALINA PUBLIC SCHOOLS

First Grade

My education in Salina public schools was fairly difficult except from about sixth grade and up. My sister was placed under Ms. Bunnel. She was a kind teacher. I don't think she ever paddled anybody. She actually came by every morning to pick up Sissy. Why she did this, I do not know. I am assuming it was possibly due to Sissy's asthma. She, in addition, knew Mom very well.

Sissy had asthma and quite frequently developed shortness of breath and wheezing, which would resolve with inhalers. With these episodes, she also usually developed shortness of breath. Perhaps this is the reason Mom and Ms. Bunnel would occasionally start talking about college. I distinctly remember Mom stating to Ms. Bunnel that I had to go to college. I had no idea what college was. Mom told me it was the place where you go after high school and become a teacher, a lawyer, a doctor, and so on. I asked her if people had to go away from home, and Mom said yes. This did not sit very well with me.

Our school was a big room that was divided in half by a curtain. Outside was a swing set, a basketball set, and a minimal area for baseball. I recall that the entire school would let out to go to a baseball or softball game at the new school. I always thought that was pretty cool. There was also a well for water. We had to pump to get the water. There was an outside toilet also. Sissy seemed to like school very much. I remember asking Mom if I had to take an afternoon nap. There was not an afternoon nap per se. There was a time after noon when we lay our heads on the desk for around ten minutes. I disliked taking afternoon naps that Mom made us do. Mom made us do this because it possibly decreased the likelihood of polio. Sissy said they had to lie their heads on the desk for about ten minutes in the afternoon.

In the beginning of school, first day, we would get assigned to either Ms. Bunnel or Ms. Eggleston. Ms. Eggleston was a no-nonsense kind of teacher that most parents as well as students did not like. We did not have air-conditioning, so kids out playing got hot and sweaty. The first day of school, Ms. Eggleston went over the rules for both inside and outside on the playground. We could put the washcloth on our forehead or neck when the weather was really hot. In general terms, the rules were as follows: Do not copy somebody's test. No fighting. Do not go off the playground. Cursing was also banned. Basically, it was reading, writing, and arithmetic, penmanship, and spelling. I recall Sissy reading to Mom every night. She occasionally had to stand up before her class and read. She was a good reader.

I was placed in Ms. Eggleston's class. Arithmetic was hard for Sissy. My first few days of school were not kind to me. I was not a good reader. I did not understand math. Within about two weeks of school, we were given a math test. There were very few questions on the test that I understood. There was a girl, Georgia Gann, who was very smart who sat the next row over from me and slightly ahead of me. Her answers I could easily see. As I was copying her answers, I did not realize that Ms. Eggleston had walked to the back of the room and was coming up my row. She had a plastic ruler with her. She slapped me on my right arm and asked me, "What are you doing?" I did not say anything. My anxiety level went sky-high. She told me to come to the front of the class. As she was pulling the wooden paddle with holes in it from her desk, she told me to tell the class what I was doing. I had to tell the class that I was copying answers on the math test. Ms. Eggleston asked the class, "Is that not one of the rules that we discussed at the beginning of school?" The class said yes, as if one has to be a real dummy to copy anything. The punishment for copying was a paddling and no recess for two to three weeks. She told me to bend over and gave me twelve slaps that hurt like hell. What an embarrassment. I told Mom when I got home. Mom said we would not tell Dad. Almost nightly, after this, Mom had me read to her. She went over math with me too. Needless to say, I did not copy again.

About two weeks later, as we were playing during recess, there was a boy who was making fun of the holes in my shoes. I chased him down and hit him in the nose with my fist. His nose began to bleed, and he went to Ms. Eggleston crying. He told her that I hit him in the nose. She asked me why I hit him. I told her that he was making fun of the holes in my shoes. As we were standing at the front of the class, she asked the class if fighting was one of the rules that we discussed at the beginning that we should not do. The class said yes. My shoes had holes in the soles. I could not help it; that was all we had. Ms. Eggleston told the other boy to go to his seat. She told me to bend over and gave me fifteen slaps with the paddle with holes in it. That one really hurt so much I was about to cry. I did not cry, however. I was so mad at the other boy I felt I could kill him. I walked out the door and went to the railroad tracks and river. I know we were not supposed to go off school grounds but what could she do? Give me another paddling? I had to do this to clear my head and regain my composure.

Again, I told Mom what happened. This made Mom so mad she went to school and asked Ms. Eggleston why there was no discipline for the other boy who had made fun of the holes in my shoes. Mom felt that he should get fifteen slaps with the paddle also. Mom asked Ms. Eggleston who was the individual who oversaw her. She told her that if there was another incident like this, she would go and file a complaint about her. Mom did talk with Ms. Bunnel about the individual who was their head. She gave Mom the name of Mr. Pierce and the phone number. Mom went to Ms. Eggleston saying that she had better have a really good reason for paddling me. "He should have other punishments rather than paddling." It was not so much me getting paddling but a situation that both boys should have been disciplined the same. Ms. Eggleston had a knee-jerk reaction to paddle the students instead of thinking things through. For instance, Ms. Eggleston paddled several times throughout the school year. I don't think Ms. Bunnel paddled at all. Was it because Ms. Eggleston had a more delinquent class than Ms. Bunnel? I think not. If there was anything good that came out of this,

I don't think that Ms. Eggleston paddled anyone else for the rest of the year.

About a week later, I followed the kid who made fun of me on the way home. I decided to follow this kid home. I told him that if he told his mother, I would beat the shit out of him. When the school was out of sight, he knew I was following him. He was afraid as I approached him. He started to run. He was no match because I was a much faster runner. I tackled him and began hitting him with my fist; his nose and mouth began to bleed. I was beating him all over with my fists. I pulled both of his arms around behind his back and proceeded to twist them as much as I could. I was hitting him in the abdomen with my fists also. The other thing I did was to shove his head into the grass and dirt. He was an absolute mess when he got home. The next day, he and his mom came to school and told Ms. Eggleston what had happened. Ms. Eggleston asked me what had happened, and I told her I had no idea what he was talking about. I told Ms. Eggleston that she had better know what she was talking about, in reference to my mother taking the situation to Mr. Pierce. Ms. Eggleston asked me if I "did this." And I told Ms. Eggleston no. Ms. Eggleston told the kid and his mother that she could not do anything if it was not on school grounds. With these two incidents, I was shunned by all my classmates. It really did not matter to me. I grabbed a basketball and went out and shot baskets during recess.

About a week later, I had to beat the kid up again. Again his mother came to school, and this time I said I did it because he was making fun of the holes in my shoes again. I stated that as long as he makes fun of my shoes, I was going to beat him up off school grounds. His mother looked puzzled. I told his mom that she was going to have to stop her son from making fun of me, and then I would not touch him. He never made fun of me again.

About midway through the school year, they were ready for us to go to the new school. Dad, Mother, Sissy, and I had seen the new school when we would go walking in the woods. It was going to be good.

Sissy continued riding to school with Ms. Bunnel. The school was a lot farther away compared with the older two-room schoolhouse. We were told to walk in single file to the new schoolhouse. That schoolhouse is still standing. It is a church at this time. The new schoolhouse now is not used because of asbestos. The last time I was in Oklahoma, I went to the schoolhouse and was able to go inside. I went to the bathroom—it still had the same smell as when I was there as a kid. I walked down the aisles, probably for the last time. I asked some people what was going to happen to the schoolhouse. The ladies told me that it would cost more to tear the schoolhouse down because of the asbestos instead of just leaving it there. The school does not have the money to tear it down, so they are leaving it as it is for now.

I did not get another paddling during my first grade. Mom helped me immensely during the remainder of my first grade. I was brave enough to tell Ms. Eggleston that I was not going to let her paddle me anymore. She looked bewildered but did not say a word. Ms. Bunnel did not paddle anybody, and there was really no reason for Ms. Eggleston to paddle anybody else in her grade also.

Second Grade

About one week before my second grade, I developed syncope because of a GI bleed. I could not stand because I would become unconscious and faint. Please see the chapter titled "Syncope." I was taken to the hospital in Pryor for the initial evaluation. They said I had profound anemia and suspected it was because of leukemia. They told Mom to go to Hillcrest Hospital in Tulsa. When we got to Hillcrest Hospital, they gave me several transfusions, which made me stronger. They ran an upper GI and small bowel X-ray and a barium enema X-ray and other blood studies. I was taken to the lab and told that I needed to take another test. They tied my hands and legs. I could tell this was not going to be a routine test. They did not give me anything to help with the pain. They took a drill and put it over my sternum and started drilling into my sternum as hard as they could. This hurt like I had never experienced in my life. When they drilled the needle in deep enough, they aspirated even more. When they got an adequate specimen, they stopped the drilling. They put a pressure dressing over the site and took me back to my room. I cried myself to sleep. I must have had a vasovagal reaction because my blood pressure dropped dramatically. A vasovagal reaction is when the body overreacts to a trigger and the heart rate and blood pressure drop suddenly. This was a very dangerous test to do if one did not know how to do it. If someone drills through the sternum they enter the cavity of the body by the aorta and heart. If one of these is nicked, the patient will more than likely die from bleeding into the chest. I left the hospital two days after this, not knowing why I had the profound anemia. They thought it was possibly an ulcer or a small polyp, which could have caused the bleeding.

They told Mom and Dad that I could not have any contact sports. They said that I needed to have a soft diet. For instance, I loved beans, but I could not have the beans. It had to be juice from the beans.

When I went back to school about three weeks after school had started, I was so far behind that I did not think I would ever catch up. The teacher gave me the lessons that I needed to learn. Probably the most difficult was learning the capitals of all the states. I took this home and gave it to Mom. We worked on all of this together, and I finally caught up. I was not reading up to the level I could be. I was also struggling with spelling and penmanship. It was embarrassing standing in front of the class and reading; the classmates would correct people if they did not know a word. I began to understand the math more. I became a better reader. The teacher would pick a student to come to the front of the class and read. As time went on, I did not dread going to the front of the room and reading.

It was always good to have Robert Sitsler on your side. He was two to three years older than anybody else. He was about 6'5". You really did not want Robert to be your enemy. He had a wicked left hook, especially with the brass knuckles. Most of the time, a dispute on school grounds was settled off school grounds. Robert, quite frequently, would come to the house to play basketball. No one could stop him in size.

At recess whatever was played, it was always "Indians versus Whites." The Indians had several good players. For the White team, it was me plus two or three others and that was it. The White team was not very good. Most of the time, we could not match the Indians. We had to make a rule that if the Indians scored five runs, then the Whites got the ball. In basketball, nobody could match my skill. I would shoot from the outside and inside very well. I would place Robert Sitsler under the basket; he was about the same size as James Chuckalock. We could score either from the inside or the outside. We therefore could better match the Indians.

If we could not play outside because of the weather, we would play marbles inside. There would be a marble that you did not want to lose. We called that a "tole." We would form a circle where there would be two to four players that would put one or two marbles in the circle, and if you could knock one or two out of the ring, those became your marbles. The other way to play would be two other players fifteen to twenty feet apart, and we would put down a marble, and if the other individual hit the marble, then it became their marble to keep. You would usually shoot with a favorite marble; it would have two to three characteristics that made that marble your favorite. You really did not want to have to give that marble up.

We tried to prevent anybody from going to a teacher because that meant we would have to stop the baseball game. We had plenty of room to play either baseball or softball at the new school. There would occasionally be a situation where the play would get heated and a fight would happen. The teacher overseeing the playground would send the individuals to the superintendent. Generally speaking, the individuals would receive a paddling and have their recess rescinded for a week or two. Academically, I felt I was doing better. I was never good in penmanship, no matter how much I practiced.

In the second grade, I started having a habit of frequent blinking of my eyes. I would do this to the extent that my upper and/or lower lid would hurt or would be irritated. Midway through the school year in second grade, the teacher sent a letter to Mom and Dad stating that she had noted that I had a bad habit of blinking my eyes. She felt that I should be seen by a doctor. She felt that it was hindering my academic performance.

Our family physician was Dr. Cameron in Pryor. Mom made an appointment to see him. There was a bus that made the trip from Salina to Pryor and back daily. That meant we had to stay in Pryor all day. When we rode the bus across the bridge's wooden planks, it felt like we were going to fall into the river. This was a horrendous, dangerous bridge. We saw Dr. Cameron, and Mom gave him the note from the teacher. After the exam, he asked Mom if there was anybody of significant influence who had the same habit. Mom said yes, his teacher. Dr. Cameron told Mom that habits like this were fairly common, and they usually went away without any consequences. Please see the chapter "My Habits." Dr. Cameron wrote a note back to my teacher and the principal. After a couple of months, that habit went away only to be replaced with another.

There were three paddlings throughout the second grade all for fights.

I spent the summer working and playing baseball. Cousin Philip was dropped off. Philip and Patty, our cousins, were dropped off for the latter part of June. Patty did this for about three summers. Philip did this every summer. Philip loved fireworks like me. Please see the chapter "Philip, My Cousin." We also enjoyed the carnival, which was in Salina, July 1–4. Philip also had a problem with habits. He also had a problem with stuttering. Mom told me that I had to read to her every day. She would have me do math every day also.

The summer went by all too fast. I felt I had a better grasp on school as compared with the last school year. I started school four weeks behind in my second year. There were no new students beginning this year.

Third Grade

Everything was harder the third year, especially math and reading. Reading in front of the class was not as hard as the last year. As I mentioned, at recess we would play softball, baseball, basketball, or tag football. Going back to the very first time that school was let out to go and watch the baseball game, this was a very favorite thing for the entire school. I was picked to play catcher the next year, which was incredible. I was a very good catcher. There was hardly anybody stealing second. The teams that we played in the area were Little Kansas, Colcord, Oaks, and more. I loved playing catcher like that. At the end of the game, everybody in my class was wanting to know about my skills as far as catching was concerned. It was quite an accomplishment. If a baseball game was Indians against Whites, there was never any shortage of Indians.

Occasionally, the Indians would have to give us one or two Indians. They were the ones that had no athleticism whatsoever. For some reason, Ronald Dry could not play. He offered to be the umpire. All agreed. When he could play, he was counted as an Indian. All of the Indians were from the Cherokee Nation. Ronald had an artificial eye. It was obvious he was cheating in favor of the Indians.

We started the third year better than the second year. We started the school year on time. I felt that my grades were just as good as the rest of the class. I will never forget when we were let out of class to go and watch a real baseball game. We had a real backstop, real bases, real pitchers' mound, and so on. The catcher had a mask and chest protector. I was so impressed with all of these. One afternoon, I told Mom and Dad at supper; their response was that I could not play catcher because I would get hurt. I told them that this catcher did not get hurt.

Little did I know that Sam Baker was starting a team during summertime to play baseball. There were going to be two different teams. Sam Baker asked Mom if I could play with his teams. Mom discussed this with Dad, and he was okay with me playing baseball with Sam Baker's team. Mom said that would be okay. Sam Baker asked Mom after church. Mom liked Sam a lot. Mom told me I could play anywhere other than catcher. Little did I know that Sam was going to put me as catcher, and I was the catcher for that team the next year.

Everybody knew that Ron was cheating in favor of the Indians. The Whites started calling him "one eye." Ron always had a purulent discharge around his artificial eye. The next day as I was walking into the school, I could see Ron and a lady who appeared to be his mother. Before too long, I heard, "My name, Warren Whiteday, and Robert Sitsler all go to the principal's office." Ron was crying. Mr. Jones asked us if we were calling him "one eye" on the school yard yesterday. We all said yes. We were asked why we were doing that. We stated because we felt that he was cheating in favor of the Indians. Ron denied this.

I walked to the schoolhouse with an Indian who stated, "You guys got cheated on a couple of calls."

Mr. Jones stated, "The most disturbing thing about this was the Whites were calling him 'one eye.'" Mr. Jones pulled out a large paddle with holes in it. He stated, "Garland, come with me." He said bend over, and he gave me twenty slaps rather hard. I was about to cry it hurt so bad. Robert and Warren received fifteen slaps. I went to the bathroom and sat on one of the stools. It hurt so bad I began to cry.

Recess was gone for a month. When I went back to class, the stinging pain was still there but not as bad as before. I told Mom about the incident. I showed Mom where the pain was coming from. She stated that she could see some bruising and swelling. That was the most painful paddling I had ever had. The month without recess helped me get caught up. I still read to Mom every night. The teacher started giving me some accelerated, harder math problems. I loved the math problems. I got most of them correct. The Indians did not know what to do with themselves during recess. I found that stopping having recess helped me immensely to get caught up and to get ahead of the class. I felt pretty good about myself as I graduated from the third grade. I had heard some bad things about the fourth-grade teacher.

About a week after school was out, I started having some abdominal pain like I had previously experienced. Milk and eating in general helped the pain. Mom took me to see Dr. Cameron. He performed an upper GI X-ray on me. I remember the films that he showed us and seeing the deformity on the X-ray. He started me on antacids and another pill. The pain was gone in one week. Dr. Cameron stated we could stop the antacid, but I should stay on the pill. The pill was to be taken around two o'clock in the afternoon. After about a week, I had no problem with heartburn or gastric pain.

The summer was otherwise uneventful. Again, Philip was dropped off in the latter part of June. His mother and stepfather went to see kinfolk in Arkansas the third or fourth of July. All of Dad's half sisters and their husbands and children came back on the Fourth of July. Dad did have a sister with whom he shared the same father, Oscar Yarborough. The other half sisters and half brother were Ruby and Jeff's children. I continued to play baseball while Philip was in Oklahoma. Baseball games or practices were in the morning. Philip and I had the afternoon to ourselves. The lake was almost filled. Philip and I walked to the boat landing almost daily.

We went with Monroe a couple of times to rescue dogs. Little did I know this was going to be Monroe's last summer. Philip got to observe us plowing gardens and the process I followed after I rescued stray dogs. I wished Philip and I could spend the entire summer together.

As soon as Philip was dropped off, we would go and get fireworks. We were not supposed to be able to buy them before July 1, but we knew the kids who had their tents on Main Street. These were children selling fireworks. We would give them a tip.

Monroe would usually give me an advance on my allowance that I would have to make up for later down the road. I never saw Philip sad. If somebody around us was sad, it would not be long before Philip would have them laughing. The summer went by very fast.

Fourth Grade

The summer went by very fast. I had been told bad things by other students. I had a very good experience in the third grade, and I wanted to carry this over into the fourth grade. Ms. Allen was a short lady who most of the time wore something black. And most of the time, she wore red shoes. She dyed her hair coal black. She always wore heavy red lipstick. By the end of the day, she had her red lipstick smeared up to her nose. What does this remind you of? Perhaps a witch. We bought a BB gun from her. She had a store on Main Street in Salina.

She loved her music. I think she wanted to form a choir for a talent show. She would sit on her stool and swing back and forth and sideways as she played the piano. We, the boys except two or three, never wanted to participate in her music endeavors. While the teacher practiced music with her group, we went to the back of the room and played marbles and shot paper wads through the straws we had gotten from the lunchroom at noontime. The best place to be was behind the coatrack. We were out of sight from her. I was learning nothing. We had no science, math, history, or spelling; it was all music. We wasted a lot of time being educated in this manner. I will say that the people in her musical group were not good in math at all.

I went to see Mr. Jones, the superintendent, and told him that I, along with a few other people, were learning nothing. I informed him that there was no science, math, history, spelling, and so on being taught. Mr. Jones had a meeting with her. I do not know what was discussed, but I do know that the music was somewhat curtailed. We started having more math, science, and spelling. This was in contrast to what the musical group wanted.

Dr. Cameron wanted me to take my medicine around one to two o'clock in the afternoon daily. I would have to go to Ms. Allen's desk and ask her for the medicine. One could see that she did not like doing this, and I did not like it either. Occasionally, she would throw the medicine at me. Mr. Jones had told Mom that if there was a problem with me getting my medication, she should notify him. Mom discussed with Mr. Jones Ms. Allen's disagreeable nature in giving me my medication; again he talked with Ms. Allen. I could tell that I was beginning to be a thorn in her side. I did not care. I would occasionally have to crawl on my hands and knees to get the medicine; how embarrassing is that? On our way to walking in the woods and fishing and hunting, we passed right by Ms. Allen's house. It was a small four- to five-room house. It was white with awnings over each window.

Halloween was payback time for her throwing medicine to me and making me crawl on my hands and knees to get my medicine. The two bodark trees in our yard gave numerous hedge apples, about as big as a softball but weighing more. The trees dropped the balls every September and October. Mom wanted the balls picked up every day in October because kids would come get them and throw them at people, houses, cars, and the like. I picked them up in burlap sacks. There were enough balls to fill three to four sacks. Sometimes people would come by and want a few balls because they thought the balls would get rid of roaches. Robert and I knew that the bodark tree limbs were limber and good for making bows and arrows. That is why we used the limbs. Dad knew this also. That is why Dad used them. The pain from a whipping with a bodark limb was indescribable. Sometimes there would be thorns, which were hard to get off the limbs. The thorns could become imbedded in the skin. Usually, a whipping was carried out with three limbs. I did not dare run. The whippings resulted in welts and bleeding anywhere the limb hit the skin.

Most of the time, we threw the balls like a baseball. They would usually not hurt the roof. We threw them at the roof and her front and back door. We could hear a lot of glass breaking from the front and back doors as well as from the windows. We threw the balls mainly at houses. I never threw one at an individual or a car, mainly because I could throw hard, and it would be some major destruction. We also threw the hedge apples at the windows at school. We broke into the high school, mainly getting racks of Coke, 7Up, and so on in the lunchroom. We fixed a sandwich along with a Coke, which hit the spot after a long hard day of trick-or-treating. We left the horse at my home. The high school was on Main Street, and seeing a horse on Main Street would make it obvious that something was happening at the high school, and we would more than likely be associated with this. We put the Coke and 7Up in a fairly safe place. We usually got home around midnight. I would get King, my dog, and fix my bed on the floor. We dreaded the next day. The damage was hard to assess.

The description of this Halloween was pretty close to what we did every Halloween. Riding the horse across her front porch was probably most unusual. That incident was the most problematic. We were lucky something bad did not happen to us.

Dwayne Sassier, Robert Sitsler, and I met before going to school as to what we were going to say about all of the damage. Obviously, Ms. Allen's house and the high school had the worst damage. I was the only one that knew how to tie the bell and the only one who knew how to untie it. Needless to say, I was told to get the bell in working order. We walked to school together. When the morning bell rang, we three were asked over the intercom to go to the superintendent's office. We were met by Mr. Jones. Interestingly, he had a hedge apple on his desk. He said that several of the teachers had these in their yard. Ms. Allen had the most and the most damage to her house. "Did you guys throw any of these apples at her house?"

I spoke first. "I could see how you would think how we were totally responsible for the damage to her house. Quite the contrary. Ms. Allen is an inept teacher, and I am learning nothing in her class. There are several kids in the class who feel the very same way, and they are afraid to talk about her incompetence as a teacher because of possible repercussions. I think you know that I have to take some medicine around 1:30 p.m. I hate to interrupt the class in order to get the medicine. Many times she throws the medicine at me. Occasionally, I have to crawl on my hands and knees to get the medicine. I think I threw three or four of the hedge apples. All of them landed on the roof. There was no glass breaking heard. I can see how you would blame all of this on us because there were a lot of hedge apples on my lawn. Lots of kids know about the hedge apples, and they will come by and get some of them. All of the hedge apples that we threw landed on the roof. They do not hurt the roof. Furthermore, all of her lights were off, and she was not giving any candy whatsoever. She would make an incredible witch." The superintendent also stated that he understood that we broke into the high school and tied the bell. I told him I would take full responsibility for that. Dwayne and Robert reiterated they too threw two to three hedge apples, and all landed on the roof. "You cannot blame us for all of the hedge apples. Several people come by and get them from our lawn." Despite all of the conversation, the superintendent stated that he was going to give fifteen slaps and no recess for two weeks. I received my slaps from the paddle first. Those fifteen hurt worse than any I had ever received. I went to the restroom and sat on the stool for about twenty minutes, crying.

For the next week, I had a problem sitting for more than ten minutes. I told Mom about the pain I was having. She looked at my buttocks, which she said was red and swollen. Looking back on this, I can see why whippings like this have been outlawed. I felt in good conscience that I could not have Mom go and talk to the superintendent because we three threw a lot of hedge apples at Ms. Allen's house. I thought about going and cleaning the lawn around her house. I could not make myself do it, mainly because of her throwing my medicine to me.

Another five to six weeks and school would be half over. So far, I had not had any more whippings, and I also felt that I had not learned much. The math and science we should have learned were not taught.

Before long, it was Christmastime. I would get so excited I would have nausea and vomiting. Sissy and I always had a good Christmas. Anything we got was from Sears, Aldins, or Montgomery Ward catalogs. I got a few things I could play with. I received books about the universe and a long telescope. President Kennedy had declared that we would land on the moon before Russia, and I received books about this. I received books about math, chemistry, and organic chemistry—all of these topics Dad and I loved to learn about. I felt that I was not learning anything at school. I would teach myself. I received books about rockets too. There was a catalog where I could order kits to build rockets. New discoveries about medicine and heart transplants were going on at Baylor College of Medicine at Houston (little did I know then that my youngest daughter would train there to be a nurse practitioner at a later date). Still, the only outside news came from the radio. I asked Dad if we could get a paper for outside information. Our library at school was nonexistent.

The kitchen table was a perfect place for Sissy and me to study. Sissy struggled with math problems, which I would work and explain to her. There was nothing to prevent us from studying when we were at the table. We would study until around eighty thirty to nine at night. There was no radio or TV to cause us to lose our concentration on studying. Furthermore, after Thanksgiving, around Christmas people would throw out their old toys for their new toys at the dump. This was a prime target where Sissy and I got new toys; many were in good shape.

In January, we started a new year. Ms. Allen told us we were going to have more math and science and so on. Furthermore, Dad instituted new rules at home—around 7:00 p.m., we were to be ready to study. If we had a game of basketball going, we would be allowed to play until dark; however, we could not have a basketball game going every day. Everybody loved a game like this. Most of the time, the men at the telephone office would come and play with us. At "study hall," we were to finish our homework and show it to Mom or Dad. Our grades were average. Being average in a Salina school was not good if you wanted to go on to college. As before, I remembered that Mom told Ms. Bunnel that I was definitely going to college.

Dad would give me extra math problems to work on the next morning. I would get up an hour early to try to work these math problems. Every Saturday, I would get a newspaper called the Grit. I had developed an interest in architecture and skyscrapers.

One Saturday in the Grit, I saw a proposal for "the tallest building in the world." It was going to be the John Hancock Center; little did I know that I would eventually live one block from this building when I was studying medicine at Northwestern.

Great strides were being made. A heart transplant was performed by Dr. Christiaan Barnard in 1967. The patient lived for only a short time. There were two surgeons in Houston that were about ready to perform a heart transplant, Dr. DeBakey and Dr. Cooley. (My daughter did see them at the hospital.) In 1969, Dr. Cooley became the first heart surgeon to implant an artificial heart; the patient lived sixty-five hours. Inventions by the two cardiothoracic surgeons were incredible.

At this time, we still did not have an indoor bathroom or any of the other amenities listed in the chapter "Poverty." We also did not have a TV. The only connection to the outside world was our radio. It was difficult to keep up with the outside world with just the radio. I asked Dad, again, if we could start receiving a daily newspaper; he stated that we might be able to do that.

With President Kennedy declaring that we would send a man to the moon, building rockets was exciting. There was a place in Denver, Colorado, where one could buy a kit to build rockets. I liked designing my own. I built a three-stage rocket, a two-stage rocket, and one that could handle a much heavier payload like a mouse or a rat. A mouse would fit into the payload of a two- or three-stage rocket without any problems.

The chicken house in the backyard had many mice and rats. I did not have any means of catching either one of these. Furthermore, I was afraid of being bitten like I had been when I was a three-week-old in my bed.

One afternoon, as I was shooting baskets, a friend of mine came over to talk to us. He said that he would give me what he had in his jacket if I guessed what it was. After three or four guesses, none of which were accurate, he pulled out a white rat. The first thing that came to mind was to shoot the rat up in my big rocket. I told my friend I would give him $0.10 for the rat; he accepted. I also bought the rat's cage for another $0.10. Mom would not let me keep him in the house. He was kept in the house that was built over the cellar. I named the rat *Sputnik* after the unmanned Russian satellite. (We would go out at night around 9:30 or 10:00 p.m. to watch Sputnik travel through space. It looked like the moon except smaller, and it was moving.) I made sure he had plenty of food and water. I would take him out almost daily. If it was going to be really cold, Mom would let me bring him in overnight. He was a good rat; he did not bite at all. He fitted perfectly into the payload of the big rocket. I shot him up in the rocket several times. I made sure that the parachute was folded appropriately every time. One afternoon, I found him dead for no apparent reason.

Finally, the fourth grade came to an end. I waited until the class had left the room. This was the last day of the fourth grade. I went up to the teacher's desk to get my medicine. She threw the medicine to me, which I caught. I told her that she was a horrible teacher and that she should be fired. I told her that I had learned nothing the entire year from her and that the information I had learned was on my own. I told her that everybody wanted to know if she rode a broom to school. She sat there stunned. The reason why she was speechless is that she knew it was all true. She came back for another year and then retired. I never said another word to her. Every Halloween, she had hedge apples thrown on her roof, through the front and back doors, as well as her windows.

The summer went by way too fast. Philip came back for three weeks. We had another summer filled with a lot of fireworks. After the Fourth of July, the fireworks were half-price. Philip and I bought as many as we could. We continued to set off fireworks with an eye out for the police. We never got caught. Money was hard to come by. We scoured the ditches for pop bottles. We found quite a few every day. We would get two cents for the small ones and five cents for the large ones. We also spent as much time as we could at the lake. I also played baseball almost daily.

At the end of the month, I was ahead of the class in reading, math, and spelling. Unfortunately, the class had to catch up to me. The teacher would give me harder math problems and reading assignments. Being ahead of the entire class really felt good. I still read to Mom as well as did math. I was still able to play basketball when I got home from school. Around five thirty, we had supper, and then I played more basketball in the backyard. Frequently, the guys from the telephone office would come over, and we would play games. We would play until dark. The wives of these gentlemen were missing their husbands. We all were very much enjoying playing basketball.

Just behind our backyard, the telephone company started building a building that would handle upgrades in the telephone system. I befriended the two men working on this project. I called them Curly and Moe; I called them these names so much that they began calling each other Curly and Moe (from the Three Stooges). They would occasionally come over and play basketball. They were listening to the World Series. I cannot remember which World Series it was.

Sometimes, there would be so many kids coming over that we would have to have three teams to play basketball. All of this was incredibly fun to everyone. This was when Mom saw the old man next door pointing a gun at us. If she had not spotted and hollered at him, he could have killed all of us. Getting his guns was something that had to be done.

Fifth Grade

When I returned to school for fifth grade, I had to listen to everybody talk about the vacations they went on. We did not go on a vacation. Indeed, we never went on a vacation. I would occasionally ask Dad why we could not go on a vacation? His answer each and every time was, "Hell son, you're on a vacation all the time now. We do not have enough money to do such things. Now get back to work."

Ms. McClay was our teacher. She did not teach music. She was a strict, no-nonsense teacher. It seemed my brain was firing on all cylinders. I was making all As. Ms. McClay was giving me extra math problems. Our library was horrible. I had no interest in reading the books that we had in the library. My athletic endeavors were also growing by leaps and bounds. I played catcher for baseball and basketball for the team in the seventh and eighth grade. For tournaments, I would be picked up by the coach. We had a very good team.

Even though I missed a considerable amount of time from class, I was able to keep up with my assignments. I was becoming recognized as the smartest and most athletic in the entire grade school—with me playing baseball and basketball like this, it left me little time to play "Indians versus Whites." Most of the time, I had to spend my time during recess catching up on assignments and doing extra work. The time that I was away playing baseball and basketball did not impair me in making all As and doing extra assignments, especially math problems. I was the best athlete not only in the entire grade school but also in the seventh and eighth grade school. I was also the smartest. I wanted and did a lot of extracurricular assignments in comparison with the rest of the class. It had been a couple of years since I had had a paddling and had not been in any fights. I felt I was learning a lot. I got along with the teacher very well.

The teacher knew I was building rockets. We were in a race with Russia to land a person on the moon as declared by President Kennedy. The teacher wanted me to bring a few rockets to the school and give a presentation on them. I did just that. I sent off a few. Everybody seemed to enjoy this, and they got a lot of information about rockets.

Playing basketball in the backyard served me very well. The Indians offered very little competition at all.

The fifth grade went by fast. Summer was filled with baseball and work. Philip came and spent three weeks. Our summer was as usual— please see the chapter "Philip, My Cousin."

One of the gifts I received for Christmas when I was in the fifth grade was a blackboard. I had no idea what Dad had in mind as I was opening the gift. When he told me we were going to do math problems using it, I was elated. Dad was excellent in math, as depicted by him being first in his class at a college in Missouri. Dad mounted the blackboard on the wall behind the front door. Almost every Saturday morning, after I had rolled 150 to 175 cigarettes for Dad, he retrieved sissy's math book; at this time, she was taking algebra, as well as the math books that I had received for Christmas in the past. Dad would read the math problems, and I had five minutes to come up with the answer. I would also have to explain how I worked the problem. Sissy was not good in math at all. We would usually do math for about one hour. Dad would want sissy to look on as I worked the math problems. Dad would usually work the math problems for the difficult ones. If there was a particularly difficult problem and I came up with the correct answer and dad did not, I would laugh and shout along with clapping my hands as I would walk into the kitchen where mom usually was. This exercise helped me become very proficient in math. I think Dad and I both look forward to almost every Saturday morning working math problems. We usually did this until the University of Oklahoma football game started. I cannot remember Dad ever missing listening to a University of Oklahoma football game. When the University of Oklahoma football started, I almost always got my basketball to shoot hoops and work on my jump shot. Around three o'clock, kids would begin to congregate to play flag football; this was such incredible fun for the kids every Saturday afternoon. Nobody ever got hurt. At that time, we did not have a television. The only connection to the outside world was our radio. I still have that radio. It is in the laundry room. I blow her a kiss every time I go by it.

There are several items throughout my house that bring back incredible memories from being a child. Some are good, and some are bad. I try to stay with the good ones.

Sixth Grade

I looked forward to my sixth grade. The teacher was Mr. Brown. He was a tall, slender man. He was an excellent teacher. He too gave me extracurricular assignments, especially in math. He knew I was playing baseball and basketball with the seventh- and eighth-grade team. He told me he enjoyed watching me play. He knew about the rockets I was building too. He wanted me to bring some to school and give a presentation too. I told him I would. He was an excellent teacher. I was never paddled by him. I was able to keep up with my assignments, making all As. Furthermore, I felt that I was learning a lot.

Seventh Grade

The seventh grade through the twelfth grade were all together on a downtown campus. The school moved into World War II barracks for the classrooms. At that particular time, they were in poor condition. There were mice and rats that were seen now and then.

There were two students in trig class—Benny Erwin and me. Benny was not in any sports. There was a teacher who did take trigonometry at the college level. He was the one who was selected to teach us trigonometry. There were mice and rats in certain areas of the barracks. We had a mouse that would come and see us around twelve o'clock.

We would also get bread every day at noon to feed the mice. We also had a gym that was in a very poor condition. We played basketball and performed plays in the gym. The out of bounds was the wall itself, and across from this were the bleachers. At the end was the entrance, and we had a concession stand at the other end of the gym. The shop was taught by Mr. Hill. He was the science teacher also. He lived across the street from us. He would occasionally come and visit Dad. They would discuss medicine, science, putting a man on the moon, and so on. Mr. Hill asked if I was still building rockets. Dad told Mr. Hill that he would talk to me. I told Mr. Hill that I was still building rockets. He wanted to know if I would demonstrate these rockets. I told Mr. Hill that I would be more than happy to do this. Mr. Hill was an excellent teacher and a very honorable man. I did put a mouse in one of the rockets' payloads. The parachute opened, and he floated back to the ground uninjured. Mr. Hill was a chain-smoker as was Dad. At recess, the teachers would congregate outside the shop and outside of the superintendent or principal's office on Main Street.

Gloria and Roy decided to move back to Oklahoma. Richard and Judy enrolled in Pryor schools, and Gary enrolled in eighth grade in Salina schools. Gloria was Dad's half sister. They moved to a three-hundred-acre farm, which they were to take care of. I was supposed to take Gary and introduce him to his room and teachers. The first to eighth grade were at a different campus, so I was not familiar with my own teachers and classroom. I was responsible for getting Gary to his classroom and teachers. I found mine without any problem. I had Ms. Jetton and Sally Cox, both excellent teachers. Everybody thought that I was kin to Jimmy Salyers because I was kin to Gary. Jimmy Salyers was kin to Roy Salyers. Jimmy and Gary were cousins. Roy is Gary's Dad. Jimmy had fairly severe mental/cognitive difficulties. Several teachers at the high school made fun of Jimmy. If it was okay for the teachers to make fun of Jimmy, so could the students. This made no difference to Steve and his despicable cronies. Steve probably had a low IQ. Steve had bad habits. I am sure that Steve's days and nights were filled with alcohol and smoking. I had a meeting with Mr. Jones and Mr. Pierce. I told them that somebody was going to get hurt in regard to Steve and his cronies making disturbing comments about Jimmy. I knew this would be met with deaf ears, especially since they themselves made these remarks. "If something happens, you have nothing to stand on legally." I believe that Steve was also having cognitive problems.

After school, Gary was to go to our house to get picked up by his mom or dad. I think Gloria did this thinking that I would try to improve Gary's grades from a C to perhaps a B. I had football practice after school. Gary was not an athlete at all. Unfortunately, I bet Roy, his father, never played any sports with him at all like my father did with me. I dreaded to go to school. I knew I would be the recipient of terrible jokes, especially from Steve and his cronies.

There was a man with cognitive deficits by the name of Jimmy Salyers. He bore the brunt of numerous jokes. He decided to go to school for a while. It became apparent that he was not receiving any benefit from school. He was told that he did not need any further schooling. He roamed Main Street, trying to get somebody to talk with him, paying visits to people working in the stores. He also frequented a cafe on Main Street and ordered a burger, fries, and a Coke. He would not drive a car. When he spoke, he would stutter and frequently have trouble expressing himself. He bore the brunt of many disparaging remarks. Most of the time, he did not know what people were saying. He knew what time recess was because he would go and smoke with the teachers. He was twenty-one years old.

Steve was so obsessed with teasing and hazing young boys; he would never tease or haze somebody his age. He stayed clear of Walter Baker, who would have stopped his teasing and hazing (fighting). I went to Mr. Pierce and Mr. Jones again, and I again told them that somebody was going to get hurt. This fell on deaf ears. I met with Gary and told him what was happening with me. He had not made any new friends.

"The school is not going to do anything. I propose that I take matters otherwise." Gary was okay with this. I told Steve to meet me at six thirty near the shop building. I had observed what time Mr. Hill left, and it was usually around five thirty to six.

I brought along a long butcher knife; I had a pair of brass knuckles. Steve immediately came after me. He threw a wild punch. I came up with a punch with the brass knuckles. I hit him with my hand with the brass knuckles. He fell to the ground, yelling and crying in pain. He began bleeding from his mouth and his nose. I grabbed my long butcher knife and yelled at the other three to "come on" if they had any problems. They began to back up. I began kicking him in the chest, hoping to break some ribs. I told them to get their crying coward. They grabbed Steve's arms and started pulling him. I had a few more knocks left in me, which made things worse for Steve. I followed these four cowards to the car. I took my long knife and punctured the back and front tires. I threw rocks through the back window and the others through the front window, rendering the auto impossible to drive. I have no idea how they got to the Pryor emergency room.

It was about ten days before Steve came to school. It was not long before he made comments again. I immediately tackled him again and started beating his jaw and nose with my fists. Mr. Jones and Mr. Pierce came out of their office, blood was everywhere, and everybody was panicking. His nose was bleeding profusely. We were taken into Mr. Jones's office. I immediately said, "Did I not tell you that someone was going to get hurt?" When Steve stood with help, I began kicking him and hitting him with my fists. I thought Steve was a coward and had decreased cognitive abilities.

The principal and superintendent were also somewhat responsible for this. The principal said, "This has got to stop." I told him that if the derogatory remarks would stop, then I would have no reason to attack anybody. It would be best if he says nothing to me.

I told Steve, "If you continue to make these remarks, you have no idea when I will attack you. The brass knuckles are lethal." His parents were called to come and get him. They were told to take him to the emergency room in Pryor. He apparently had a fracture in his jaw. He missed another week of school. This didn't mean anything for him because he was cognitively impaired. Interestingly enough, my mom was good friends with his mom and Steve's sister was good friends with my sister. His sister died after a surgical procedure at a Pryor hospital in the twelfth grade. When Steve returned to school, I think he was embarrassed about what had happened to him.

I again went to talk with them about what happened to him. I reiterated to them, "Did I not tell you that somebody was going to get hurt?" They told me that anyone who got caught making derogatory remarks about Jimmy would be punished. Not too long after that, Gary transferred to Pryor, where his brother and sister were going to school. In addition, Jimmy was sent to a long-term care facility. This was the appropriate place for Jimmy since nobody was looking out for his welfare. Otherwise, the derogatory remarks regarding Jimmy were essentially nonexistent.

Eighth Grade

The summer between my seventh and eighth grade, Richard Crawford and I went to a baseball camp. It was an excellent camp. Please see the chapter "Baseball Camp."

The first ten days of eighth grade, I went to West Texas for a funeral. Roger wanted me to go with him. Roger had worked at the Salina school system for a year. He fell in love with my sister, Sissy. Our mom and dad liked Roger, and they trusted him. He was like family. I had never been on a road trip like this. Roger had worked combining for the last two semesters. He worked for an individual who died of malignant melanoma. This was a common medical problem in the area because people would combine or plow for ten- to twelve-hour days without any sun protection whatsoever. Roger also thought it would be educational.

Mr. Hill and my father got into heated debates about some subjects. Both were chain-smokers. I was gone for about eight days with Roger. Everybody in school wanted to know if I was coming back to school. Ms. Jetton and Sally were our main teachers. They were both excellent teachers. They would give me extra work to do, mainly math problems. Again, the library was nonexistent. I had received books at Christmastime for the last two to three years and basically taught myself about a lot of the subjects.

One day after lunch, somebody at the back of the classroom challenged me to arm-wrestle with James Chuckalock. James was about 6'5", well-built, not fat, a lot of muscle. He was a jovial guy. He never got mean. Somebody offered a $1 for whoever won. James and I positioned our chairs to get started. When we started, his hand was bigger than mine. One minute was gone, two minutes were gone, about three and a half minutes had gone by. At about four and a half minutes, I could tell he was getting tired. At five and a half minutes, I beat him. I collected my dollar and class began. The class could not believe what had just happened. The teacher wanted to know what had just happened. He was told I beat James in arm wrestling; he was stunned also. They did not know that I had been swinging an ax all day on weekends as well as doing biceps and triceps exercises with a big heavy sledgehammer that I got out of the junk pile (the pile where Sissy and I got toys went "viral").

Mrs. McClay decided we should have a party to socialize with our fellow seventh- and ninth-grade students. Mrs. McClay gave me a list that needed to be filled and told me to bring a cake. I went home and told Mom that we were going to have a party and that Mrs. McClay told me to bring a cake. Mom said, "Sonny, we do not have an oven." Anxiety hit me like a ton of bricks. Oh how I dreaded to tell Mrs. McClay that we did not have an oven. She reassured me that it was okay and that I should just bring something to drink. Mom only had kerosene burners. We did not have a refrigerator and running hot water. We had a box that we could put a chunk of ice in to keep things cool but not a refrigerator. There was an ice house on Main Street that would deliver blocks of ice, putting it on the porch. The block of ice went into a container, which kept things cool. It had no electricity. It melted by the next day. The items could stay in the box for perhaps twenty-four to thirty-six hours, and then they had to be thrown away. We got a block of ice daily; however, I really hated poverty. We did not have an indoor toilet or any of the other items listed above. I was still sleeping on the floor. At this point, I understood that we were poor.

I felt that I was learning a lot academically and sports-wise. I had played with the ninth-grade teams even in the sixth grade. I liked my teachers; they frequently gave me extra work to do. Some very interesting things were happening. Russia had already put a satellite into orbit. Dad and I would go outside to watch *Sputnik* almost every night. I remember one night it being five degrees Fahrenheit. This was between ten and eleven o'clock that *Sputnik* would pass by into orbit in October of 1957. This was really the beginning of the race to the moon. In his speech, President Kennedy said we should put a man on the moon before Russia. It looked like the moon except that it was smaller and moving. I had received a telescope as a present, which I would take outside when we went to see *Sputnik*.

There was also a lot going on in Houston regarding a heart transplant. The first transplant was by Christiaan Barnard in South Africa. The patient lived for only a very short time. There was also a lot of research going on by Dr. DeBakey and Dr. D. Cooley both at Baylor College of Medicine in Houston. There was Dr. Shumway at Stanford also. It is unbelievable that my youngest daughter would graduate from the University of Texas with her nurse practitioner degree at Baylor in Houston. There was a lot of work in cardiothoracic vascular research at Baylor in Houston.

I asked Dad if we could get a newspaper. He said he would look into this. I really needed to have one or two papers for outside information. This was eventually accomplished, and it was great!

Ninth Grade

Academically, I think I was learning a lot. The following teachers were excellent: Ms. Jetton, Mr. Hill, Ms. Cox. Most of the information I was learning was from the books I got at Christmastime. Our school library was nonexistent. Most of the books were old.

We did not receive a newspaper. Ms. Cox would give me extra math problems. Mr. Hill and Ms. Jetton would give me world events to write about. We could select a topic to write about. Again, this was limited because of our library or lack thereof. Most of the information was in my books or in the local newspaper. Mr. Hill would walk to our house to talk about current events. Mr. Hill thought Dad was a very intelligent person even though he quit school after the ninth grade. I would agree. Mr. Hill wanted me to talk to my class about rockets. This was followed by me shooting off some of my rockets. Mr. Hill was getting ready to shoot off a rocket. There was a sharp pin that was given to me to set off the rocket. I put the pin in my mouth, and unfortunately, I swallowed it. I could tell that Mr. Hill was both mad and concerned. He was concerned that the pin would make a hole in my gastrointestinal tract. The pin was passed probably after about thirty-six to forty hours. I never had a problem, such as severe abdominal pain. About three days later, Mr. Hill came to the house and told Dad about this. Dad thought the pin had passed also.

Mr. Winfield was an excellent basketball coach. He also coached football and baseball. We, the ninth grade, were undefeated in both football and basketball. Butch was an excellent athlete also. He was point man for our basketball team. If we could have James Morrison, Tommy Powell, me, Butch Winfield, and James Chuckalock, along with two or three other players, I felt we had a very good chance to win the state in basketball. Mr. Winfield was an excellent coach, especially with basketball.

One Saturday night, Mr. Winfield was taking the basketball boys and girls to regional play. They would both go to state if they won. That afternoon, Butch and I were riding his scooter on the highway. He asked me where I wanted to go. I told him since we were out by our eighty acres, I was going to leave it up to him as to where he wanted to go. He said he would like to go where Joyce lived. I replied, "Let's go." The scooter did well on the highway. We went to the door and rang the doorbell, and Joyce came to the door.

Joyce was a girl that everybody would like to date. We were there about an hour. We knew we had to be in front of the gym if we were going with them, the team. We thought that we had enough time after an hour; we decided to head back home. As we left the driveway, we hit a big pothole. Butch thought we would make it through the pothole. We did not make it. The front end locked, and Butch was thrown over the scooter. I was underneath the scooter. My entire body was in the pothole full of water. I was concerned about the exhaust burning my leg. This necessitated us to contact Mr. Winfield to tell him to come and get us. He was mad as hell. Thank goodness we made it out of there in a small pickup truck. He put the scooter on the truck. As for me, the scooter had fallen on the left side of my body. My leg was okay—no cut or burn was noted on my left lower leg. We quickly got the scooter into the bed of the truck. Butch and I rode in the bed of the truck, making sure the scooter was good. My dilemma was what I was going to do with my shoes. There was a cut and a hole in my left shoe with my white socks shining through the cut—it looked horrible. This was so embarrassing. I put black shoe polish on my sock, which helped somewhat. Both of the games were incredibly good. The girls had Joyce Winfield and another tall girl with an incredible hook shot. They won and were going to the state. Now, it was the boys' turn. They had an excellent team with a very good center. It went down to one shot, which was missed. Everybody was stunned. We had been ahead by six points late in the game, and it slipped away.

We went to the secondhand store the next day, and I got a decent pair of shoes. These, at least, did not have holes in them.

Mr. Winfield wanted to become a superintendent. He preferred the Salina school system, but he could also go to the Little Kansas school system; this was all left up to the school board. The other individual who was being considered was Mr. Jones. It took hours of deliberation. Eventually, the word came down that Mr. Jones was their choice. This was devastating to Mr. Winfield. I was sure he would have stayed at Salina. Mr. Winfield was eventually hired at Adair. They had both academics and athletics. There he stayed until he retired. Roger Klinger was hired at Adair school also. He too stayed at Adair until he retired. From what I understand, Adair had a better school system, academically as well as sports-wise. I am sure Mr. Winfield had a hand in this. When Mr. Winfield was in high school at Salina, the ninth-grade football team was just before high school football. Coach Winfield wanted me to stay around for punting. I could kick the ball a long way. Mr. Winfield wanted me to punt for home games. I tried to punt the football in a spiral because it would go farther. I also kicked the ball very high such that the defense had a good chance of getting to the player who was supposed to catch the ball.

Roger decided to go to a St. Louis Cardinals baseball game, taking both me and Butch. Butch brought some Red Man chewing tobacco; he asked if I wanted any. I said sure, I would try. I had never done this before, never smoked a cigarette, and so on. I took a good-sized chunk of chew. I was warned about not swallowing the juice or any of the tobacco itself. Too late!I had swallowed the solid as well as the liquid part of the tobacco. I felt horrible with dizziness, difficulty with walking, terrible dry heaves. I got in the car and lay down on the back seat. We had to stop and get a pail for my nausea and vomiting. The next day, I felt a lot better. I was eating better. I was able to go to the ball game. I promised I would never try chewing tobacco again. Part of the big chew. The feeling was kind of the feeling that I would get when I rolled 125–150 cigarettes for my dad with Prince Albert tobacco on a Saturday morning.

My kicking I learned when Bobby Baldridgee and I would do a lot of kicking and receiving the football. We could kick the ball about the same distance.

Roger had something to do around Little Kansas and wanted to know if I wanted to go. "Sure," I said. It was about school. As we drove up to Butch's house, I could see that he had a yellow Mustang with black interior. This was given to him by his mom and dad because he would be commuting back and forth to Northeastern College. Giving their son a car meant they were wealthy compared with us. I was glad for Butch; we were always good friends. We spent a lot of time together. We could not afford a newspaper.

Lee Iacocca, head of Ford Motor and Chrysler, developed and designed the minivan and the Ford Mustang. At that particular time, the auto industry could not put out enough minivans and Mustangs to supply the demand. He borrowed a large sum of money from the feds and paid it back in a very short period of time. The other two auto companies came out and said that they did not need three automobile companies in the United States. Chrysler paid back the money in record time. The Ford Mustang and minivan were Lee Iacocca's babies. They could not be made fast enough. I would have given a lot to have a Mustang in high school.

Tenth Grade

Mr. Winfield went to Little Kansas as the superintendent. We had won the football game and the girls' and boys' basketball games in Salina. Mr. Winfield had to see the Little Kansas team go down to a loss. We won the conference games. I was scoring 25–30 points a game. There was hardly anybody who could stop me, or our team. Yes, I was the starting center for the tenth-grade team. That year, we had a good center for ninth and tenth grade—that was me. For regional play, we won a game against a team from Tulsa. The next game, we lost. I feel that we should have another good team for the next school year. I very much enjoyed playing for Mr. Winfield in the ninth grade. I was looking forward to playing for him in the tenth grade.

Little did I know he was going to Little Kansas and then to Adair as superintendent. I also very much enjoyed playing with Butch. Little did I know that Mr. Winfield was working with the center for Little Kansas to block my shots in basketball. I had my way with almost anybody on the court when I was in the tenth grade. That's how I was able to get 25–30 points a game. I made "first team" all-conference, center, also all-district. Little did I know that the basketball team was planning ways to keep the ball from me because they could not stand the notoriety I was receiving.

In the tenth grade, in football, the coaches would evaluate tenth graders to see if they could be of any benefit to varsity football. I just got to the field for the evaluation of the tenth graders. I was chosen first. I could tell it was a chosen play to see what I would or could do with Steve. He was halfback and I was safety. I could tell that it was a set play. Basically, the play was for me and Steve to hit as hard as we could. We both bowed our helmets and hit as hard as we could. My helmet had slipped from him in a major impact to his shoulder. I hit him as hard as I could. Steve started crying and yelling as loud as he could. He was lying on his back, moaning and yelling. The other thing I heard was Coach Harten yelling at me, "You're going to start there Friday night," over and over and over. I had not seen Coach Harten so jubilant over something. As I was getting up, Steve was still on the ground, yelling in pain, as I could see he was complaining of chest and shoulder pain. I took several steps with my cleats on his lower extremities. As I started walking away, the two coaches were helping him to stand. I was probably twelve to fifteen yards away. I turned and ran as fast as I could, putting my helmet into his chest. I knocked down not only him but also the two coaches. Hack told another coach to grab me and march me off school grounds after I got my books and clothes.

There were years dating back to when I was in sixth and seventh grade, when I played up two years, Steve loved to haze me. Steve was taken to the hospital in Pryor. They saw a small fracture of his jaw. Also, he had a fractured clavicle on his left side. Steve, again, I think, was embarrassed in regard to football and baseball. He missed a week of school again. I don't think it was going to make much difference since I felt that his cognitive faculties were limited. I really think the only difference between him and Jimmy Salyers was that one had parents and the other did not.

Steve missed the entire football season. He really was not missed at all. I took his place in football at halfback and played safety also. I played one side, and Richard Johnson played safety on the other side. Academically, I was learning information that I thought was going to be good. However, I had nothing to compare this with. I just did not think that academics at Salina had anything to brag about.

The next sport was basketball. Salina had lost an excellent center because of graduation. Everybody was wondering if I could be as good as Jim Hoag was at center. I made first team center, and my game improved game after game. I was making 25–30 points a game. I could play center, but also a few of my points were from rebounding and back up again. We had an excellent team. We were one game from going to the state. I made all-conference and all-district in both baseball and basketball. I don't think that sat too well with some players and parents who received no notoriety.

This was Coach Davis's first year. I enjoyed basketball as a sophomore. I would get a lot better going into my junior year. However, little did I know that the team, superintendent, principal, players, their mothers/ fathers, and the school board were all against me. (See eleventh-grade basketball.)

The next sport was baseball. I continued to be the catcher. We had a good team but nothing great. We had one good pitcher, but beyond this, the pitching was questionable.

Eleventh Grade

My junior year, we were projected to come in first in basketball and baseball and have a high showing in football. I was a preseason favorite as to why we would come in first in basketball and baseball. In football, we went to one game postseason and lost. After football, I was looking forward to basketball. I had an excellent season the year before and was looking forward to another. I was bigger and stronger and ready to play. I got an excellent write-up in the preseason paper.

Unfortunately, there were several people who had other plans for me. After a couple of games, no one was passing me the ball. I was scoring 6–8 points per game, whereas as the previous year I had been scoring 20-plus points per game. We were losing games that we should have been winning. People in Salina and referees were asking why nobody was passing me the ball. I think that the majority of the people knew why I was getting ostracized from the team. In essence, we were playing with four players. After five games, we had not won a game. The only way I was scoring was loose balls and rebounds. I asked Coach Davis what was going on. He lied to me and told me that he did not know. The refs that loved to watch me play asked me why they were not passing me the ball. We knew why. They were jealous of the degree of notoriety I would have been getting if they did pass me the ball. This was the reason. If Mr.

Winfield, my ninth-grade coach, would be the coach, this would not be tolerated. He would have played without a team rather than adhere to their wishes; and when I say this, I'm talking about the superintendent, the principal.

By midseason, I was ready to quit. If it had not been for two or three people, including Roger Klinger, I would have quit. We found out later on that the jealousy extended to the superintendent, the principal. I think that these two or three people, including Roger Klinger, gave me wrong advice. I think they should have told me to quit in the middle of the season. There were also some school teachers who were very jealous.

This was Mr. Davis's second year in coaching. He was carrying out what the school board and others wanted. Mr. Davis did not have the balls or spine to do the right thing. He was a mediocre coach anyway. Davis heard that I was thinking about going to another school. He told me in no uncertain terms would he not allow me to play with another school. A school with a very good basketball program met with my father one Saturday night and presented several incentives if we would move there. Please see Eleventh Grade Basketball. The coach stated that they had been watching me play. "We were at four different games recently." They wanted us, my family, to consider playing for this other team. (I will not name the school.) "We think this is a travesty, what they are doing to your son. He is easily all-state material. This school has a reputation as an excellent basketball program. They also have very good baseball but no football program." I was so much looking forward to going to another school, preferably to the first school. I did not want to play sports for Salina or any of the coaches. Not only this, but I did not want to go to school at Salina. Furthermore, this other school had much better academics compared with Salina public school. Don Brown, Lonnie Stevens, and Richard Johnson all carried out these scandalous orders with jubilation. They would rather play like this, poorly and lose, than win the conference like we should have. The team and coach, as well as the school board, would rather lose than pass me the ball. Indeed, we had lost all of our games, extending to ten at that time. We were supposed to be come in first place, whereas about halfway through the season, we were in last place. Halfway through the season, I was wanting to quit or go to another school. Davis told me that he would not allow me to play with another team. Indeed, Davis would rather me play with a sinking ship instead of me playing with a real team and real coach.

I was glad when basketball was over. I still think that I should have quit basketball and told Coach Davis that I would not be playing baseball. In baseball, I did hit a home run to propel us into postseason play. Mike Haley was able to play baseball as a junior. He continued to receive radiation for his testicular cancer. He was our starting third baseman.

I played sports without any enthusiasm at all. Coach would tell me to hustle. I would tell him, "This is the best I can play. If you have anybody else that can play, I'm gone." There were a lot of pass balls to the backstop. If there was anybody on first base, I would not try to throw them out. Most of the time, they would steal second and third bases. I don't think I threw anybody out over stealing all year. The other players could sense my lack of enthusiasm. They would all tell me things, which I ignored. There was very little communication between us. Coach Davis pulled me aside after I hit the home run that propelled us into postseason play and told me that he was trying his best to get me all-state. I looked him in the eyes and told him he was full of shit. "You might as well stop now. You are wasting your time. I can't think of another team that did this to a player on the same team. If there was another situation like this, tell me. You have no idea how much I wanted to transfer to this other team. You have no idea how much I did not want to play for you." I began to cry. "You have no idea how much I wanted to quit!"

Roger and I talked about this several times; him telling me to continue to play was the biggest blunder Roger ever told me. "Furthermore, this other team has much better academia compared with Salina. You told me that you would not allow me to play with another team. We would sue you and Salina public schools, and you would not like what I would say about you and Salina public schools. The superintendent, the principal, and the school board, and I think you know who on the school board sealed my fate not to make all-state. You guys made sure of that due to unprecedented jealousy. Shame on each and every one of you! You have no idea what you put me through. You need to be thinking about someone else to play catcher next year. I'm really thinking about not playing sports for Salina next year." Coach Davis just stared at me as if he knew he had made a big mistake. I pulled off my shin guards and threw them on the ground and started walking home.

It was a long walk home, but I did not care. It felt good to be by myself and to clear my head of what had just happened. I walked home slowly; it took me about an hour. I went to the hay house and lay there for about an hour. The dogs loved when I went and lay down with them in the hay house. They gave me unconditional love. All of them were just about dead when I found them and rehabbed them back to an incredible life.

Football—eleventh grade

I continued to play halfback and safety. We were to have a very good team. We lost only two players from the previous year. We were still undefeated about halfway through the season. We were playing Colcord. I was playing safety on defense. There was a play to the opposite side. As I was looking to the opposite side, the end came up and hit me with some object in the head that was very hard. He hit me with his right arm. I was unconscious for three to five minutes. The coach came out, and they hauled me off the field. When I woke up, I remembered what happened as well as who had hit me. When I woke up, I was ready to go back into the game playing safety and halfback. Hack told me a little later I told him, "Either you put me back in, or I will walk onto the field and cause a penalty from having too many players on the field." Hack reluctantly put me back in. There had been three plays that went on while I was on the sideline.

Two plays later, there was a pass to their end right on the out-of-bounds mark. The pass was a little high, necessitating him to jump a bit. This was a perfect position for him to be in as I placed my helmet into his abdomen. I also was about fifteen yards from him. This gave me the perfect position to hit him as hard as I could in the stomach. When I hit him, he yelled out in severe pain. I could feel his entire body go limp. I told the ref that he had something hard on his right upper extremity. Indeed, his right upper extremity was wrapped with something very hard; this was what he hit me with a very hard wrap, not sure what might have been in it. The ref saw what it was. He talked to the coach for Colcord, who had to know that he had some object on his right upper extremity. The ref told the coach that they were going to have to forfeit the game. The player was still in severe abdominal pain. He was carried off the field. I never saw the player again. I found out the next day that he broke my helmet. This had to be a very hard hit in order to do this.

Basketball—eleventh grade

We were projected to be conference champs. Only two players had graduated. It was Coach Davis's second year. Little did I know that the team was going to try to keep the ball away from me as much as they possibly could. As a sophomore, I had averaged 25–30 points a game. I was first team in all-conference and first team in all-district in baseball and basketball. Now the only way I could score was with a rebound. We had played four games. We had lost all four games. I went to Coach Davis and asked him what was going on. He replied, "I don't know. I am looking into this." In reality, he did know. He did not have the fortitude to stop what was happening. I know Mr. Winfield would not have put up with them not giving me the ball. I think Coach Davis knew all about this. This was something that came from the top, that is, the school board. There were three players, seniors, who decided to make sure I did not get the ball, and they were okayed by the school board, superintendent, and principal. It did not matter if we won or lost the game. Everybody was willing to forgo a potentially excellent basketball season just to prevent me from having an excellent season. What I should have done was to quit basketball and play no more sports.

Teachers would ask me what was going on. I told them, "I do not know. Ask the superintendent."

My dealings with the superintendent in the past depicted him to be a very honorable and fair man. He knew exactly what was happening; his son was on the team. I lost all respect and confidence in him.

The refs would come up to me and ask me what was wrong. My reply was the same. They would comment, "Hang in there."

One Saturday night, I was sitting by the two windows in the living room. We were getting ready to listen to the *Grand Ole Opry.* The shades were drawn, so I could not see outside. I could hear cars parking. It sounded like they were parking in front and to the side of the house. Soon, I heard people walking on the porch. After that, there was a knock at the front door. Mom and Dad were in their usual positions on the couch. I looked at Mom and Dad, and they said to answer the door. I did. The people wanted to talk with my father. Dad got up and went to the porch. Why they wanted to talk to Dad, I could not come up with a reason. I had not been in any recent fights or had any other problem with the law. This group consisted of superintendent, principal, the coach, mayor, and three schoolteachers. They talked for about an hour. I will not specify the town that the people were from. The bottom line was that they wanted me to come play sports with them, mainly basketball.

They had an excellent basketball program. They thought my addition would give them a chance to win the state title for a couple of years. They were probably correct. The school did not have football. (Football was a sport that I could easily forgo.) They had a good baseball program too. The school was academically much better than Salina. The coaching in baseball and basketball was much better also. They would also give Dad a job if he needed one. They would give Mom a job. They would give Mom and Dad transportation if and when they needed it. They would give Mom and Dad a newer house to live in. They would give Mom and Dad money if needed, within reason. Dad told them that he was going to have to think about this and discuss it with Mom. I think they were both stunned about this. The coach asked me to come and play some basketball with the team. I went four different times. The team was (good?) beyond expectation. The coach thought we played very well together. He thought we could win state for two years in a row. Somehow Coach Davis found out about this. Probably from the refs. Coach Davis had lost all credibility to me. I did not want to play any sport for him and certainly not for Salina. The coach called me into his office and wanted to know what was happening. I told him that I did not want to play a sport for him or Salina. At this point, I didn't know what I was going to do. Coach told me he was going to do everything he could to make sure I received all-state. I told him that I really did not care. I told him that I was going to do whatever I could to transfer to another school.

Roger Klinger was also devastated. He was a good friend to Coach Davis, and up until this happened, another coach in our conference wanted me to go to his team and play. He looked into this, having me live with his parents. There were three other schools that inquired about me coming to their school. I so desperately wanted to go to another school. I begged Dad to accept the first school that wanted me. I was devastated when Dad told me we could not move. I began to cry. I told Dad he was stealing my dreams form me. "Do you remember all of those days when I played basketball in the backyard by myself? There were numerous times I dreamed about playing with a good team, and we would play in the state tournament and win. My reward would be all-state. This is it, Dad. This is it. Salina basketball does not deserve what I could have given them. There were so many people that loved to watch me play. Now, I have no desire to play any sport for the coaches or any desire to go to school at Salina. Dad, please reconsider the first proposal. You saw what kind of team we would have." I left to go shoot hoops in the backyard.

I was so glad when basketball was over. We won one game the whole season. I still think that I should have quit basketball and told Coach Davis that I would not be playing baseball. In baseball, I did hit a home run that propelled us into postseason play. Mike Haley was able to play baseball as a junior. He continued to receive radiation for his testicular cancer. He was our starting third baseman. I played sports without any enthusiasm at all.

This ruined my sports as well as my studies. I did not play sports for about three weeks. The team won only one game during that time. I came back to baseball where I hit a home run to propel us to the playoffs. We lost the first game.

Twelfth Grade

The summer between my junior and senior year was unprecedented. I tried to forget what happened to me my junior year. I asked Coach Davis to give me the name of another individual that was treated this way; he could not. I did run to the bridge toward Locust Grove almost every day. This was about seven miles round trip. I usually dove off of the bridge and swam to cool off; it felt so good. I did not run and swim to get in shape for sports at Salina. At that particular time, I was seriously contemplating not playing sports my senior year. I ran because it made me feel good. I ran with five-pound leg weights on each leg also. What happened to me my junior year was so repugnant that I really did not care to play for any of the coaches or for Salina public schools. Furthermore, I did not want to go to Salina public schools. What they did to me was unforgivable. Not going to another school was devastating to me.

There was a form that had to be filled out for me to go to college. One day, when I was going by the principal's office, I asked if this had been filled out. It had not been filled out. If I did not turn in this form, I would lose my exempt status—students with a premed major were exempt from the draft as long as they carried a grade point average

(GPA) of 3.0 (out of 4) or better. I had to go to Pryor to fill out a form every semester. I told the principal to quickly fill this out and I would mail it that day. I really felt that the principal intentionally did not fill this out because I did not want to go to Northeastern College. Instead, I enrolled at OSU. I felt that there was unprecedented jealousy. Just because nobody from Salina public schools had ever graduated from OSU or OU did not make it impossible for anybody else to graduate from OSU. I immediately got the filled-out form and mailed it. I think the principal and my counselor were in cahoots to sabotage my enrollment at OSU. Four years later, I made certain that the principal and my counselor knew that I had graduated from OSU with a 3.8 grade point average and that I was accepted to medical school.

After graduating from Salina public schools, I never saw or talked with these two atrocious individuals ever again. Furthermore, I took the hardest courses OSU had to offer. These were subjects one had to take to be premed. As time went on that summer, the urge to play sports my senior year increased. Furthermore, Mike Haley was talking to me about trying out for sports. Running to the bridge all summer put me in good shape. We did not have a weight room. The chapter "Left Knee Injury" describes what happened, sports-wise, my senior year.

I could not believe I was injured in the first football game. Things got better with rest and exercise. Again, in the first basketball game, I reinjured my left knee, which led to surgery. The basketball team did not win a game until I returned halfway through the season.

Baseball, basketball, and football were played without a great deal of enthusiasm for each sport. I could not wait for graduation. After surgery on my left knee, I developed deep venous thrombosis, which delayed my second surgery for three to four weeks. I had the second surgery by Dr. Coker. I was discharged on a Sunday and started class that next day, Monday.

My academic studies my senior year at Salina public schools were status quo. My education at Salina public schools were inept in preparing me for premed at OSU. I took the hardest classes that Salina public schools offered. I was senior class president. I spent a lot of time organizing senior class trip and Chouteau day. There were five boys who took physics with Bob Piguet. Instead of classwork, we spent most of the time taking pictures and developing them in the darkroom. We also did a lot of hunting and fishing. We had a lot of fun with Bob Piguet; however, we did not learn a lot of physics. When Mike and I jumped over the "threshold," the front two doors to the school, I never went back. That really felt good! The bell was never tied at Halloween again.

CHAPTER 37

Water Witching

Dad bought forty acres about six miles away from Salina. He bought it very cheap from Sylvia, one of his half sisters. They were in financial distress and needed to sell it. They, at one time, wanted to build a house on the forty acres.

Dad decided to buy a house and move it onto the property. This house was over toward Pryor, Oklahoma (by this time, there was a good bridge over the lake replacing the dangerous bridge). It was a two-story house that had to have a portion of the top removed because of the low-lying electrical wires in Salina. The foundation was already in place. We needed to get the roof on before it rained. I was helping to get the roof on when I stepped on an area that I thought was stable. I stepped there, and much to my surprise, it was not stable. I caught myself with my hands and arms. If I had fallen all the way to the ground, that could have spelled disaster. Next, we needed a water supply. Grandpa Jeff Dobbs was in town; Sylvia and Bud, Dad's half sister and her husband, came over on a Sunday. Dad asked them if they could ask Jeff to come over and "water witch" a well for the house. On the way over, Jeff got a forked peach limb from Grandma's house. It was about twenty inches long. We all went to the house that had been moved onto the forty acres.

I was not a believer; I had to see for myself. Jeff started near the house, mainly in the back. There was nothing. He started again, near the front of the house, where he was probably twenty-five to thirty-five yards away. Here he found what appeared to be a good area. He went east, west, north, and south. I could see the peach limb pointing to a certain area anyplace he went. I watched Grandpa Jeff's arms and hands; they did not move at all.

I tried it, and it would not work for me. Dad tried it with the same result as mine. The thing that was very telling was the bark was stripped off of the peach limb.

Before too long, Dad hired a man to drill the well. He too was a believer in water witching. He started drilling, and about sixty feet down, he hit water. It appeared that the depth of the water source was excellent. Most people would say that this is "hogwash." I have seen only one well that was "water witched." The peeling of the bark from the peach limb was very telling to me. Furthermore, the well that was witched was an excellent one. Could we have drilled anyplace else and come away with the same good well? For me, I believe in water witching.

I had to dig a ditch four feet deep, all the way around the back of the house. This was brutal work with all of the rock and roots I encountered.

The well was a good one. The people that lived there never ran out of water.

ABOUT THE AUTHOR

Garland Yarborough, MD, FACG, FACP, is a physician board-certified in internal medicine and gastroenterology. He is a graduate of Oklahoma State University with a degree in physiology. He is also a graduate of Wake Forest Medical School. He did an internship and residency at Northwestern University in Chicago, Illinois, for three years, followed by a fellowship in gastroenterology at Vanderbilt in Nashville, Tennessee, for two years. He is the author and coauthor of several papers studying the effects of different drugs on the coronary circulation in dogs. During his fellowship in gastroenterology, he is the author and coauthor of several papers studying the effects of drugs on hepatic function. He is also the author of a paper comparing the findings of rigid proctoscope with that of fiberoptic flexible sigmoidoscopy. These findings gave credence to the benefit of colonoscopy in the screening of individuals for colon cancer. Dr. Yarborough lives on a farm with his wife, Linda. His farm has served as a home for numerous rescue animals and still does. Dr. Yarborough and Linda have five wonderful children and six grandchildren. Three of his children are in the medical field: Hope, a nurse; Brandon, a pharmacist; and Ashleigh, a nurse practitioner. Garland Jr. works for a company he founded, and Zach is a system analyst technologist.

www.ingramcontent.com/pod-product-compliance
Lightning Source LLC
Chambersburg PA
CBHW060913120626
46553CB00001B/314